"This workbook could not be timelier as an invaluable resource for the growing number of people who struggle with anxiety and depression—especially as we battle an unprecedented global health crisis. Michael Tompkins masterfully explains psychological theory and integrates evidence-based interventions into easily applied strategies for reducing emotional pain, improving functioning, and facilitating values-based living. Numerous real-life examples lend validation to reduce shame and illustrate effective implementation of skills."

—**Rochelle I. Frank, PhD**, assistant clinical professor of psychology at the University of California, Berkeley; adjunct professor at The Wright Institute; and coauthor of *The Transdiagnostic Road Map to Case Formulation and Treatment Planning*

"The main idea of cognitive behavioral therapy (CBT) is that we can feel better by practicing new habits of thought and behavior, and there is a wealth of evidence to back up this idea. In *The Anxiety and Depression Workbook*, Michael Tompkins walks you through the steps of CBT, including challenging negative thoughts, mindfulness, reducing avoidant behavior, problem-solving, exposure, and self-compassion. Tompkins speaks to the reader in a manner that manages to be comprehensive yet also highly accessible. It's like having a master therapist at your side as you read. If you suffer from anxiety or depression, this is the book for you. I'll be recommending it to my clients for years to come."

—**David F. Tolin, PhD**, director of the Anxiety Disorders Center at the Hartford HealthCare Institute of Living, president of the Association for Behavioral and Cognitive Therapies (ABCT), and coauthor of *The Big Book of Exposures*

"If you are seeking evidence-based tools and strategies to help you cope with anxiety and depression, I urge you to read this book. Michael Tompkins is an experienced and talented clinician who has used these strategies to help thousands of individuals. If you read this book, he can help you too."

—**Jacqueline B. Persons, PhD**, director of the Oakland Cognitive Behavior Therapy Center; and clinical professor in the department of psychology at the University of California, Berkeley

"This excellent workbook contains a wealth of practical information, presented in easy-to-understand language; complete with graphs, worksheets, and practice exercises. All is designed to help distressed persons *act* in the face of their anxious and depressed feelings—rather than avoid them. Conceptually, the focus is on teaching a variety of skills to build emotional, cognitive, and behavioral flexibility. Learning these skills will enable the reader to create lasting change that will reduce distress and improve quality of life."

—**Dolores Gallagher-Thompson, PhD, ABPP**, emerita professor in the department of psychiatry and behavioral sciences at Stanford University School of Medicine, practicing geropsychologist, and internationally recognized researcher in dementia family caregiving

"If you struggle with anxiety or depression, you should read *The Anxiety and Depression Workbook*. Written by a very seasoned clinician, it offers a coherent set of strategies for managing these emotional concerns that are based on contemporary clinical science."

—**R. Trent Codd III, EdS**, executive director of the CBT Center of Western North Carolina, and coauthor of *Socratic Questioning for Therapists and Counselors*

The Anxiety *and* Depression Workbook

Simple, Effective CBT Techniques to Manage Moods and Feel Better Now

Michael A. Tompkins, PhD, ABPP

New Harbinger Publications, Inc.

Publisher's Note

This publication is designed to provide accurate and authoritative information in regard to the subject matter covered. It is sold with the understanding that the publisher is not engaged in rendering psychological, financial, legal, or other professional services. If expert assistance or counseling is needed, the services of a competent professional should be sought.

NEW HARBINGER PUBLICATIONS is a registered trademark of New Harbinger Publications, Inc.

Distributed in Canada by Raincoast Books

New Harbinger Publications, Inc.
5674 Shattuck Avenue
Oakland, CA 94609
www.newharbinger.com

Cover design by Amy Daniel

Acquired by Tesilya Hanauer

Edited by Marisa Solis

Library of Congress Cataloging-in-Publication Data

Names: Tompkins, Michael A., author. | Beck, Judith S., author.
Title: The anxiety and depression workbook : simple, effective CBT techniques to manage moods and feel better now / by Michael A. Tompkins, PhD, ABPP, Judith S. Beck.
Description: Oakland : New Harbinger Publications, 2021. | Includes bibliographical references.
Identifiers: LCCN 2020038389 (print) | LCCN 2020038390 (ebook) | ISBN 9781684036141 (trade paperback) | ISBN 9781684036158 (pdf) | ISBN 9781684036165 (epub)
Subjects: LCSH: Anxiety--Treatment. | Depression, Mental--Treatment. | Cognitive therapy. | Anxiety--Problems, exercises, etc. | Depression, Mental--Problems, exercises, etc.
Classification: LCC RC531 .T662 2021 (print) | LCC RC531 (ebook) | DDC 616.85/2206--dc23
LC record available at https://lccn.loc.gov/2020038389
LC ebook record available at https://lccn.loc.gov/2020038390

Printed in the United States of America

23 22 21

10 9 8 7 6 5 4 3 2

For Lu

Contents

Foreword

Why should you read this workbook? If you suffer from anxiety or depression, or know someone who does, you'll find it quite valuable. In the 1960s, my father, Dr. Aaron T. Beck, developed cognitive behavioral therapy (CBT), and since then, researchers, clinicians, and policy makers worldwide have recommended CBT as the psychological treatment of choice for anxiety and depressive disorders. At the Beck Institute for Cognitive Behavior Therapy, we have taught tens of thousands of clinicians how to improve their effectiveness by using the techniques in this workbook.

During the past ten years, researchers have studied what we have observed: emotional disorders share important core factors that maintain anxiety and depressive disorders, regardless of the disorder or the diagnosis. And one of the primary factors is emotion avoidance.

In *The Anxiety and Depression Workbook,* Dr. Michael A. Tompkins suggests that if you suffer with excessive anxiety or depression, the treatment is straightforward: decrease your emotion avoidance by enhancing your emotional flexibility. Greater emotional flexibility sets the stage for approaching rather than retreating from your anxious or depressed feelings, and thereby builds your tolerance to these uncomfortable emotions.

In this book, as in his other books, Dr. Tompkins translates complex psychological concepts into practical yet highly effective skills. You'll begin by learning to record your anxious and depressed experiences. In addition to identifying the thoughts and actions that maintain your emotion avoidance, you'll identify the ongoing consequences of avoiding your anxious and depressed feelings.

Next, you'll learn mindfulness and acceptance skills that will add flexibility to your attentional system. What you attend to and what you ignore contribute to your emotional inflexibility. This inflexibility makes it difficult for you to shift your attention in order to see situations and yourself as they really are.

Then, you'll learn skills to think more flexibly. These cognitive change strategies are a core feature of cognitive behavioral therapy, and Dr. Tompkins describes several simple-to-use thinking skills that set the stage for the emotion exposures that follow.

Once you've loosened your emotional system through the application of the mindfulness and thinking skills, you will move to the essential step of building your emotion tolerance through emotion exposures. Although facing your emotions may seem counterintuitive, you'll soon learn that approaching rather than retreating from your anxious and depressed feelings is the key to a fuller and more meaningful life. In this book, you'll learn to do this.

In addition to skills to build emotion tolerance and flexibility, you'll learn skills to build gratitude and self-compassion. In true CBT fashion, these skills shift your attitude. For example, you'll learn skills that focus on what you have rather than what you lack, as well as self-compassion skills to counter the self-criticism that is a part of excessive anxiety and depressive feelings.

The skills in this book are potent. I encourage you to try each one, either on your own or with the help of a therapist. Nearly a half century of research demonstrates that these skills and techniques work. If you want to live with a greater sense of well-being, I encourage you to read *The Anxiety and Depression Workbook* and learn and practice these skills.

—Judith S. Beck, PhD
President, Beck Institute for Cognitive Behavior Therapy
Clinical professor of psychology in psychiatry, University of Pennsylvania

Part I

Understand Your Emotions and Prepare to Change

Chapter 1

What Is Emotional Inflexibility?

If you suffer with excessive anxiety or depression, then you likely feel intensely anxious or down more often than other people. When you're anxious, you feel like the volume knob is turned too high; your mind is racing and your body is tense. When you're depressed, you feel like the volume knob is turned too low; your mind is slow and your body is heavy and tired. And, once you're anxious or down, you tend to remain in these emotional experiences while others recover and move on. In other words, your emotional system may have *less flexibility* than other people's systems. And this makes it hard for you to bounce back from anxious and depressed feelings and do the things that help you live the life you want.

Emotional flexibility is the ability to respond to life's challenges with an appropriate level of emotion, and then to recover as these situations change. A flexible emotional system is perhaps the single most important feature of psychological health. Fortunately, the flexibility of your emotional system isn't fixed—it's plastic. And you can enhance the flexibility of your emotional system if you work at it.

The goal of this workbook is to teach you skills to increase your emotional flexibility. With a more resilient emotional system, you'll feel less anxious and sad, and better able to bounce back from the ups and downs of life.

The skills in this workbook—such as *mindfulness*, *flexible thinking*, and *self-compassion*—are the same skills that you'd learn in *cognitive behavioral therapy* (CBT). CBT is the gold standard for the treatment of anxiety and depression. More than fifty years of research tells us that these skills help people recover from excessive anxiety and depression. Whether you're anxious or depressed, or suffer with an anxiety or a depressive disorder, or both, this workbook is for you. One workbook, one program to follow, and one set of skills to learn and practice. That's because both excessive anxiety and depression reflect an inflexible emotional system.

An Inflexible Emotional System Is the Problem

Albert Einstein defined insanity as *doing* the same thing over and over and expecting different results. When it comes to emotions, it's about *thinking* the same things and *paying attention* to the same things over and over, too. This inflexible habit of thinking, acting, and paying attention leads to anxious or depressed feelings that are disproportionate, distressing, disruptive, and persistent.

Inflexible Attention

Attention plays an important role in our emotional responses. If you're walking down the sidewalk and you hear a sound coming from the alley, you'll assume (although you're not certain) that the sound is danger. Once you make that evaluation, your attention will shift to the sound in order to identify whether it is a threat. Similarly, if you make a mistake, your attention will focus on thinking through what you did in order to learn something that will help you solve the problem if it arises again. This is all normal.

However, excessive anxiety and depression are maintained by a particular type of attention: *biased* and *inflexible*. If you're overly anxious, you tend to focus on threats (or what you perceive as threats) rather than on safety. For example, you might overfocus (*biased attention*) on the dangers of flying and overlook the fact that flying is much safer than driving to the airport. If you're depressed, you might overfocus on the negative (or what you perceive as negative), even on very small negatives. For example, if your friend tastes the soup you made and then says, "The soup is wonderful but it could use a little salt," you might hear only "could use a little salt" and not "wonderful."

Not only is your attention biased toward threats and negatives, once your attention shifts to a threat or a negative, it's very difficult for you to shift back. Your attention is *inflexible* in the same way that you're thinking is inflexible. In fact, when you suffer with emotional disorders, your attention is often so inflexible that it's difficult for you to see the world around you as it truly is.

Inflexible Thinking

When you struggle with excessive anxiety or depression, you tend to interpret things in inaccurate, unhelpful, and inflexible ways. For example, you might overestimate the likelihood that bad things will happen, or overestimate the impact of an event and then feel anxious throughout the day. You might overgeneralize, such as taking a small mistake and concluding that you're a failure, then feel hopeless and down. These thinking patterns are automatic and inflexible. In fact, you often don't even realize that you've fallen into them.

Learning skills that help you first recognize that you've slipped into these thinking patterns, and then help you shift out of them, are essential to recovering from excessive anxiety or depression.

Inflexible Action

In addition to inflexible thinking and attention, you likely have *inflexible action* too. These are the habitual actions you take to avoid or control feeling anxious or down. Sticking to "safe" topics for fear of saying the wrong thing, or repeatedly checking locks because you're afraid someone might break into your home, are examples of *anxiety-driven physical actions*. Avoiding activities that you once enjoyed because you feel too tired to try them, or spending hours in bed because you're too overwhelmed to go to work, call a friend, or even take a shower, are examples of *depression-driven physical actions*.

You likely also use mental actions to avoid feeling anxious or down. However, unlike physical action habits, mental action habits are all in your head. For example, with *anxiety-driven mental actions* you might repeatedly reassure yourself that you didn't hit someone while riding your bicycle, or repeatedly analyze a past conversation to convince yourself that the person liked you, or at least didn't dislike you. *Depression-driven mental actions* include repeatedly going over events in the past that didn't go well. For example, asking yourself repeatedly why you received a good but not excellent job performance evaluation and then criticizing yourself because you "should" have done better.

An Inflexible Emotional System Leads to Avoidance

Figure 1.1 illustrates the typical cycle that an inflexible emotional system throws you into. A challenging life event happens; you respond by thinking in the same ways, acting in the same ways, and focusing on the same things. This emotional inflexibility amplifies your emotional responses to life's challenges. And gradually, because you feel intensely anxious or depressed, you avoid the events and situations that trigger these strong emotions.

For example, if you're depressed, you might avoid socializing because you think that you won't enjoy it. Or if you're anxious about your health, you might avoid visiting your doctor because you fear bad news, or avoid exercising if you fear that exercise might cause you to have a heart attack.

Typically, you avoid negative emotions, such as anxiety or depression, but you might avoid positive feelings, such as happiness or joy, too. For example, if you're depressed you might avoid positive feelings because you think that you're not worthy of positive experiences, such as laughing with friends. Or you might avoid pleasant activities because you believe that enjoying yourself means something bad will happen because you've lowered your guard.

As you repeatedly and automatically avoid or escape normal but potentially uncomfortable human experiences, you become less tolerant of them. Soon you begin to believe that you can't tolerate feeling anxious or down, and this belief further fuels your wish to avoid what are uncomfortable but natural emotional experiences. As you continue to avoid, it becomes more difficult to lean out of these emotional experiences to see life as it truly is.

So here's the bottom line: when you consistently avoid your anxious or depressed feelings, you don't learn that you can tolerate them as you pursue the important things that make life worth living.

To summarize, inflexibility in the way you think, act, and pay attention are core features of excessive anxiety and depression. This inflexibility causes you to avoid your emotional experiences, and this avoidance creates an emotional system that doesn't bounce back when you experience the ups and downs of life.

The skills in this workbook will increase the flexibility of your emotional system and, in the process, build your tolerance to emotions such as anxiety and depression. Learning that you can tolerate your anxious or depressed feelings is how you recover from the uncomfortable feelings that are limiting your life.

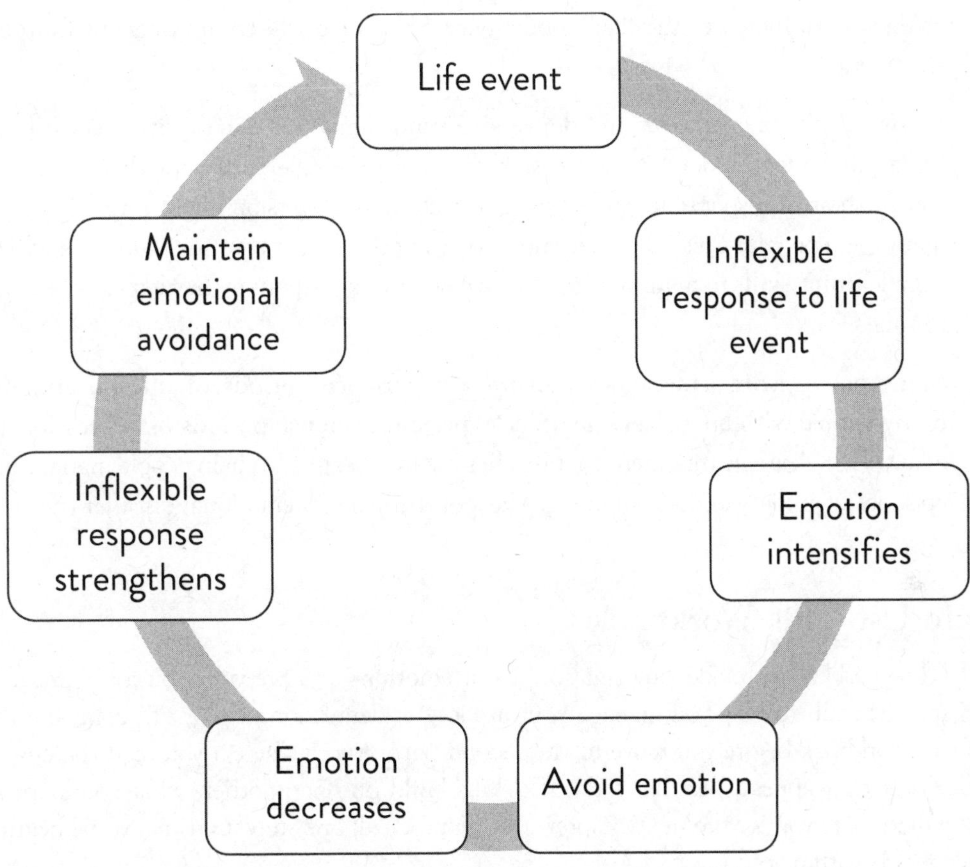

Figure 1.1. Emotion Avoidance Cycle

Transdiagnostic Treatment for Anxiety and Depression

During the last few years, researchers have developed new treatments that target core factors believed to maintain symptoms of excessive anxiety and depression (Moses and Barlow 2006; Allen, McHugh, and Barlow 2008; Taylor and Clark 2009; Norton and Paulus 2016). These new treatments are called *transdiagnostic treatments* because they are effective whether you have a diagnosis of an anxiety or depressive disorder, or both (Farchione et al. 2012; Ellard et al. 2010). There are several advantages to a single treatment for anxiety and depressive disorders:

- **Many people with an anxiety disorder also have a depressive disorder.** For example, the co-occurrence of anxiety disorders and major depressive disorder is as high as 60 percent (Kaufman and Charney 2000). A single treatment that works for both anxiety and depressive disorders simplifies recovery. A limited and effective set of skills, whether you're anxious or depressed, increases the likelihood that more people will try and benefit from a single treatment.

- **Many people have anxiety and depressive symptoms that don't quite meet full criteria for a particular anxiety or depressive disorder.** A single treatment that targets central factors thought responsible for excessive anxiety and depression might improve the lives of many more people. This is because those who do not have an emotional disorder still benefit from learning skills to manage the excessive emotional responses they experience from time to time.

- **Many people with a depressive disorder experience periods of intense anxiety, and many people with an anxiety disorder experience intense periods of depression** (Regier et al. 1998). A single treatment that teaches common skills can help people manage periodic episodes of anxiety or depression regardless of the primary emotional disorder they have.

How to Use This Workbook

Part I of this workbook provides information about emotions and prepares you for change. Part II teaches specific skills to help you manage your anxiety or depression. It's best to complete the first part of this workbook before you move to the second part. And it's best if you read the chapters in the order that they appear. All the workbook skills build on one another; what you learn in one chapter will prepare you for the next chapter. As you proceed, one step at a time, you'll begin to see that recovery is within your grasp.

The overarching goal of this workbook is to develop and cultivate a new and more effective attitude toward your emotions. This healthier attitude toward your feelings will come out of the skills in this workbook, which are well tested. But like any skill, they only work when you apply and practice them. And when you put in the work—as you practice the skills—and are better able to tolerate your emotional responses, you'll begin to notice that your emotional system is more flexible and that flexibility enhances and opens your life.

To learn and practice the skills in this workbook, you can download free copies of nearly all of the worksheets (and some audio recordings) at this book's website, http://www.newharbinger.com/46141. These online accessories are identified throughout this book with the following icons: 🗎 for worksheets and 🔊 for audio recordings. They will also help you to organize and track your learning.

The work you'll be asked to do in this book can change your life. And like all life-changing journeys, you'll run into challenging bumps and detours. So it's important to set up your foundation: support and health.

Gather Your Support Group

Sometimes it can be difficult to ask for help or support. But seeking support from trusted friends and family members is a powerful public statement that you're ready to work on your recovery. And having support often gives you the best possible chance to master the many skills in this workbook.

On the lines provided, list friends, family members, or professionals who would be good members of your support team. Include their telephone numbers and email addresses:

____

____

____

____

____

____

Having a therapist on your team is valuable, particularly if the anxiety or depression has created a significant life crisis for you, such as losing your job or an important relationship. If you're repeatedly thinking of killing or hurting yourself, immediately contact a therapist who specializes in the treatment of depression.

Remember, depression is a treatable problem, and with guidance from a mental health professional and the skills in this workbook, you can recover and feel better. If after learning and practicing the workbook skills you're still struggling, you may want to meet with a therapist.

If you're already meeting with a therapist, take this workbook to your next therapy appointment and together look through it. Discuss the skills in this book that you think could help you recover from your anxiety or depression. You and your therapist may want to discuss at each meeting your progress learning and practicing the skills. If you run into a problem with a skill, together troubleshoot a solution to get back on track.

See Your Physician First

If you haven't told your physician about your anxiety or depression, tell your doctor before you start working through this book. Your physician will likely want to conduct a thorough examination to rule out medical conditions that are similar to or exacerbate symptoms of anxiety or depression. For instance, if you often feel tired in the morning and have trouble concentrating throughout the day, these might be symptoms of depression—and they could also be fueled by hypoglycemia, or low blood sugar. Also, medications and over-the-counter drugs can create anxiety-like or depression-like symptoms, as can some of the foods you consume. For example, excessive caffeine can cause you to feel anxious, and excessive alcohol can cause you to feel down.

In addition, your physician might recommend that you meet with another medical specialist for further evaluation. Follow through with these recommendations until you and your physician are confident that your symptoms are due to excessive anxious or depressed feelings and not a medical problem.

List the names and contact information of your primary care physician and medical specialists who treat you. Describe the current medical conditions for which you are receiving treatment and the medications (if any) your doctors are prescribing for each condition:

____

____

____

____

____

____

If You're Taking Medications

People who have struggled with chronic anxiety and depression often take medications in order to feel better and to get through the day. If you're already taking medications for your anxiety or depression, you can continue medications while using this workbook. However, certain medications, such as benzodiazepines (Ativan, Klonopin, Xanax, Librium, Tranxene, and Valium), taken every day can dampen your emotional responses so that you don't get the full benefit of the skills in this workbook, particularly when building your emotion tolerance (see chapter 8).

However, unless your physician recommends it, don't increase or decrease the dose of your medication while working through this book. If your physician recommends that you try a new medication, postpone working through this workbook until you reach a stable therapeutic dose, and then start or restart the workbook program. It's better to keep your medication the same while working through this book so that you fully benefit from the skills you learn and practice. In addition, if you change medication while working through this book, you might not know what is helping more: the medication or your hard work.

If, after you finish this workbook, you want to decrease your dosage or stop it all together, talk to your physician first. Together you'll develop a plan to decrease your medication slowly while your physician follows your progress.

Finally, if you begin to use more than your usual amount of medication as you work through this book, particularly if you're taking more anti-anxiety medication than normal, this might signal you require more support. Alert the physician prescribing your medication that you're using more, and seek a consultation with a mental health professional experienced in treating anxiety or mood disorders. If you're already in therapy, ask your therapist to coach you through the skills in this workbook. With a bit more support, you'll be able to stabilize your medication usage and continue your recovery.

Long Story Short

Everyone on occasion feels anxious or down, but when your anxiety or depressive symptoms are overly distressing, disruptive, and persistent, you may be suffering with an emotional disorder. Regardless, whether your symptoms are moderate or severe, if you struggle with anxious or depressed feelings from time to time, this workbook can help.

The objective of this book is to teach you skills that target the factors thought to maintain your excessive emotional responses to life's challenges. As you begin working through this workbook, remember:

- Inflexibility in the way you think, act, and pay attention is a core feature of excessive and persistent anxiety and depression. This inflexibility causes you to avoid your emotional experiences, and this avoidance maintains the intense and persistent emotional responses you have to life events.
- A single approach that targets the primary factors that maintain excessive anxiety and depression simplifies what is necessary for you to learn, remember, and practice.
- The goal of this approach is to enhance your emotional flexibility by learning and practicing skills to shift and modify your thoughts, your attention, and your actions. Enhancing your emotional flexibility will lessen your emotion avoidance and enable you to live a full and meaningful life.

Chapter 2

Anxiety and Depression

At times, we all feel anxious and sad. We also feel other uncomfortable emotions such as anger, guilt, and shame. These are normal human experiences—just as normal as feeling contentment, surprise, happiness, and love. Emotions are good because they serve a specific purpose. Emotions motivate us to act in ways that help us not only survive in the world but to thrive too. These emotion-driven motivations or actions are automatic and helpful, because when we feel something we do something.

Anxiety tells us to prepare for future threats or dangers. *Fear*, on the other hand, is about immediate threats. There's very little thinking involved in fear. It's automatic because, when faced with real and imminent danger, it's better to act first and think later.

Sadness is a natural emotional response to a situation that we can't correct or resolve, such as the loss of a loved one or a personal or professional setback. This inability to control or resolve the situation creates a sense of hopelessness or extreme dejection. Sadness directs us to slow down and withdraw, so that we can process a loss or think through a failure and learn from it. Sadness or *depression* also signals to others that we're in need of help and support.

So, yes, emotions are good. Emotions help you cope with the hard knocks of life and learn new ways of responding if you encounter them again. Emotions are useful because they enable you to adapt to your circumstances—at least, when your emotional system is flexible.

How Emotions Become Emotional Disorders

An inflexible emotional system is the definition of an emotional disorder. But what turns a flexible emotional system into an inflexible one? To answer that question, it helps to understand that there are two emotional responses at work: primary and secondary.

Primary Emotional Response

The *primary emotional response* is the first emotional response you have to a new event or situation. For instance, imagine that you're in an elevator one day. You push the down button, the doors close, and the elevator starts to move. Suddenly, the elevator jerks and stops. Your body tenses, your heart beats faster, and your attention focuses on the perceived threat: the elevator. Is it still dropping? Your primary emotional response is fear.

In a few seconds, the elevator begins to move again. At your floor, the doors open and you step off. At this point, you realize that you're out of danger or realize that you weren't really in danger. Your primary anxious response begins to dampen. Your body and mind calm. You call the building manager, who sends a maintenance crew to check the elevator. Your primary anxious response worked perfectly, kicking in to help you when it was possible that you were in danger, and subsiding when it turned out you were not.

In the case of depression, your primary emotional response is sadness following a loss or a setback. For instance, imagine you're in sales and you lose a big account. For the next couple of days, you repeatedly think through what you could have done differently. Perhaps you could have followed up sooner with the customer or lowered your quote a little more. When you realize what you could have done but didn't, you think that you're a lousy salesperson. You feel guilty that you let down your team. You notice that you're having trouble concentrating at work and that you're less motivated to make sales calls. You wonder what's the point of trying and leave work a little early.

Secondary Emotional Response

Your *secondary emotional response* follows the primary emotional response. This response is normal and natural too. It's composed of the same components (thoughts, physical sensations, attention, and action). But where the primary emotional response is acute, in direct response to the situation that triggered it, the secondary emotional response lingers. The secondary emotional response prepares you for the possible return of the threat or for the continuation of the problem. However, once the threat has passed or the problem resolves, this secondary response fades—when it's flexible.

Remember the elevator? At the end of the day, you head out of the office for the elevator but hesitate at the door. Your secondary emotional response is in charge. You're still a little anxious. You consider taking the stairs, but the elevator doors open and you watch colleagues step in. Everything looks fine—no danger, no threat. You step into the elevator and press the down button. Your body is tense and your palms are sweating a little. You stand near the door rather than near the back because that feels safer. As the doors close you listen carefully for any unusual sound. The elevator continues down. It doesn't drop. All is good. The elevator then stops and the doors open. You step off and your mind and body quickly calm.

However, for the next few days, each time you step into the elevator, you feel a little anxious. Day by day, however, your anxiety lessens. After a while, you find yourself daydreaming on the elevator, the way you used to, not thinking about whether the elevator might drop again. This is your secondary emotional response in action—and because it's flexible, it adapts to the reality of the situation. Your thoughts, your attention, your physical sensations, and your actions return to what is normal and appropriate. This is your secondary emotional response at its best.

When it comes to sadness, the process is the same. Remember that lost account? The next day, although not feeling 100 percent, you're feeling better. You're still thinking about how you let down your team, but you remind yourself that everyone loses a sale. As you enter the building, you smile at your colleagues and they smile back. You make a couple of sales calls and you're back on track. By the end of the week, you're feeling like your old self.

Stuck in an Inflexible Secondary Emotional Response

As you can see, secondary emotional responses are as adaptive as primary emotional responses—most of the time and for most people. This secondary response only becomes a problem when it's stuck in a pattern that is difficult to change. People who have anxiety or depressive disorders have secondary emotional responses that are inflexible, at least about certain objects, activities, or situations. Their secondary emotional responses tend to linger, which cause them to avoid their feelings and the events and situations that trigger them. This persistent avoidance only worsens their emotional inflexibility until it becomes more difficult to go about their day-to-day activities, work toward important life goals, and enjoy their lives.

For example, you might have an emotional disorder (for example, a phobia) if, after the event in the elevator, you begin to avoid that elevator and then all elevators because you worry excessively that the next time you ride an elevator it might indeed crash to the ground. This is an inflexible secondary emotional system that isn't bouncing back. It's stuck in the process of thinking and avoiding, as if danger is around the corner in spite of evidence that elevators are safe.

Similarly, you might have an emotional disorder (for example, major depression) if, after the setback at work, you continue to dwell on the setback, repeatedly criticize yourself, and pull back from activities because you feel too depressed to do them. You stop exercising or spending time with friends. Perhaps you begin to overeat or drink. This too is an inflexible secondary emotional response. You're stuck in thinking and avoiding long after most others bounce back.

These disproportionate emotional responses to life events can persist over time, sometimes for years, and eventually culminate in anxiety and depressive disorders. In a sense, people with emotional disorders are trapped in an inflexible emotional system, and a central feature of that inflexible emotional system is avoiding anxious and depressed feelings along with the situations linked to these feelings. The approach in this workbook is to build a flexible emotional system that enables you to recover from the following emotional disorders.

Anxiety Disorders

Anxiety disorders differ from the everyday anxiety that we all feel because the anxiety is more intense, lasts longer, and interferes significantly with day-to-day functioning. Although about 5 percent of people in the United States have one of the following anxiety disorders, you might be one of the 8 percent (Brown and Barlow 2009) of people with symptoms who don't fit neatly into one of these diagnostic categories. This workbook can help you too. Furthermore, the skills in this workbook will help decrease your anxiety and stress in general, even if you don't have an anxiety disorder.

Panic Disorder

People with *panic disorder* experience panic attacks or a wave of intense fear or terror that causes distressing sensations such as some combination of shortness of breath, racing heart, nausea or stomach distress, choking or difficulty swallowing, dizziness or lightheadedness, sweating, feelings of unreality, or feeling detached from oneself. During a panic attack people may fear that they're dying, going crazy, or losing control. People often experience panic attacks as coming out of nowhere. They have strong urges to escape or leave a situation, although they're not in danger. Once people begin to experience panic attacks, they worry about future panic attacks and may avoid certain situations and activities.

Mateo is a successful attorney who prides himself on working harder and longer than any other attorney in his firm. During the last few months, the firm lost several big accounts, and the senior partners were pressuring Mateo and the other attorneys to bill more hours. Also, last month Mateo and his wife had their first child, and neither Mateo nor his wife is sleeping well because of the baby. Adding to Mateo's stress is his wife's persistent requests that he spend less time at work so that he can help with their newborn.

One morning on the way to work, as he rode the escalator up from the subway to street level, he had his first panic attack. Mateo clutched the handrail tightly because he felt intensely dizzy and short of breath. He was terrified that he would pass out and fall. He ran the last few steps off the escalator in a panic. He managed to work through the day, but during the next few weeks he began to have panic attacks in other situations, such as when walking upstairs, when riding in the subway, and when driving over certain stretches of highway.

At first, the panic attacks felt as if they came out of the blue, but over time Mateo began to worry that he may feel intensely dizzy at any time and in any situation. Mateo continued to ride the subway but only to street-level stations that did not require him to ride an escalator. He began to avoid other things, such as stairs, balconies, and multistory parking garages. Mateo tried several things to "control" his panic, such as breathing and medications. However, Mateo continued to avoid the situations that triggered the physical sensations that frightened him and, as a result, each month his world grew smaller.

If you think you may have panic disorder, describe on the lines provided why you think this is true:

____

____

____

____

____

____

Generalized Anxiety Disorder

People with *generalized anxiety disorder* experience excessive and uncontrollable worry about everyday things, such as their health, relationships, money, or world events. They often worry about little things, such as getting to places on time, or bigger things, such as completing a work project. People with generalized anxiety disorder tend to worry much of the time, which creates ongoing stress and physical sensations, such as muscle tension, nausea, and headaches. They often have trouble focusing or sleeping. People with generalized anxiety disorder find it difficult to stop worrying, even when they're trying to do other things.

Nia describes herself as a "part-time nanny and full-time worrier." She worries about the same things other people worry about, but she worries too much and for too long. She works part-time because she feels overwhelmed by her anxiety and worries. She doesn't sleep well. The moment she lies down, she starts worrying about the things she needs to do the next day.

Her biggest worry is about her relationship. She worries that her boyfriend will dump her at any moment, even though the relationship is good and he repeatedly tells Nia that he loves her. She feels irritable much of the time and argues with her boyfriend over little things.

Nia has chronic headaches and diarrhea. She would like to find a different job, but every time she thinks about looking she worries that she'll never find something—and then puts off looking. Most troubling, Nia can't stop worrying when she wants to stop. She feels powerless because she believes that she can't delay worrying, even for a few minutes.

If you think you may have generalized anxiety disorder, describe why you think this is true:

____

____

____

____

____

____

Social Anxiety Disorder

People with *social anxiety disorder* (social phobia) experience intense fear of negative evaluation by others. They experience intense anxiety in social or performance situations, such as when meeting people they don't know well or when giving a presentation at work. When people with social anxiety are in these situations, they may even have a panic attack. They tend to avoid social or performance situations, or get through them but feel very anxious and will leave if they can.

Rosario has always been anxious about speaking in front of people. She worries intensely and excessively that people won't like her or that they think she's incompetent, particularly when she's in front of a group. She also feels this way when talking to people she respects or in positions of authority, such as the principal at her school. Rosario experiences little anxiety when teaching younger children. However, when budget cuts forced her to take a job teaching high school, she began to dread entering the classroom.

One day, while lecturing to her class, Rosario began to blush intensely on her face and neck. She felt unable to continue speaking and left the classroom. She started to worry that this would happen again, so she began to call in sick when she felt too anxious. She also started to avoid wearing certain colors because she feared the color would make her face look red. She also started to wear heavy makeup to hide the blushing.

Rosario missed many days of school but managed to get through the school year. Over the summer, she began to think that she isn't cut out to be a teacher, even though she loves teaching and teaching is the only thing she has ever really wanted to do.

If you think you may have social anxiety disorder (social phobia), describe why you think this is true:

____

____

____

____

____

____

Obsessive-Compulsive Disorder

Although *obsessive-compulsive disorder* is no longer classified as an anxiety disorder (American Psychiatric Association 2013), it still shares several features with anxiety disorders, notably emotion avoidance and inflexible thinking, attention, and actions.

People with obsessive-compulsive disorder experience *obsessions*. These are frequent unwanted or irrational thoughts, images, or impulses that don't make sense to them. Horrific or aggressive images may pop into their minds that are very disturbing. They may intensely doubt that they turned off the stove or locked the front door. Because these thoughts create intense anxiety or fear, people try to suppress or neutralize them with ritualized actions or thoughts. These physical or mental actions are *compulsions*. They may repeatedly check that the stove is off or that the door is locked. They may pray over and over in their head. They may wash their hands repeatedly.

People with obsessive-compulsive disorder will also avoid activities or situations that trigger the obsessions or compulsions. They may avoid touching objects because they fear coming in contact with dirt or germs. They may avoid driving because they fear they'll hit a pedestrian with their car. They may avoid moving items in their rooms because they don't want to have to move the items back and forth until they feel okay.

Malik is a chemistry graduate student. He's started to repeatedly wash his hands anytime he has the thought that he has touched something that might have germs on it. When he washes his hands, he does it in a specific and elaborate way, to make certain he doesn't miss a spot. He begins with the small finger on his left hand and moves up and down the inside of the finger to the next finger. The process typically takes forty-five minutes.

And the longer he washes, the more anxious he feels. Many times Malik stops washing only because he can no longer bare the pain in his shoulders or the loud and angry protests from his roommate, who wants to use the bathroom. The thoughts of germs and images of getting sick frustrate Malik because they don't make sense—he knows those thoughts are irrational—but he can't ignore them or get them out of his mind.

If you think you may have obsessive-compulsive disorder, describe why you think this is true:

____

____

____

____

____

____

Major Depressive Disorder

A major depression differs from the sadness we all feel when we experience a loss or setback in life. In fact, "depression" is a clinical term to describe intense and persistent feelings of sadness and despair. That said, *major depressive disorder* is one of the most common mental health conditions in the United States. One in ten adults has had at least one major depressive episode (Hasin et al. 2017).

People with major depressive disorder, or what most people describe as depression, feel very down or blue on more days than not. They're no longer interested in things that once interested them, such as watching sports or going out with friends. They often eat too little or too much, and have trouble sleeping or sleep too much. They have difficulty concentrating and often feel sluggish or slowed down. They have little motivation to do things. They may feel guilty or worthless, or think that life is meaningless and the future hopeless. They may have thoughts of hurting or even killing themselves.

Janine is struggling after her fifteen-year marriage ended eight months ago. She cares for her three children and works part-time as a cashier in the restaurant her family operates. When not with her kids or working, she stays in bed and either sleeps or binges on junk food. When her friends or family members call or drop by to visit, she doesn't answer the phone or door.

Janine once enjoyed scrapbooking with friends, but she no longer feels like doing it. She drags herself through each day. She feels exhausted but has trouble sleeping. She is often irritated with her children and can't concentrate at work. Janine feels guilty that she doesn't enjoy being a mother anymore and blames herself for the marriage failing. She has had periods of feeling down or sad in the past, but she's never felt this depressed for this long.

If you think you may have major depressive disorder (depression), describe why you think this is true:

____

____

____

____

____

____

Basics of Emotion

Although predisposing factors, such as genetics and early upbringing, can play a role in the development of your excessive anxiety and depression, and life events can precipitate a major emotional episode, there's not much you can do to change your biology or always prevent difficult life events. However, you can change the way you think and act, and what you focus on. Every emotional experience, such as anxiety and depression, includes thoughts, physical sensations, attention, and actions (see Figure 2.1). In the remainder of this chapter, we'll look at each of these components and learn how they interact to influence and maintain your anxious and depressed feelings.

Thoughts and Images

When you're feeling sad or depressed, you often have thoughts about events that you cannot correct or control, or about a situation you believe is hopeless ("What's the point of trying? I'll just screw up again"), or that you're inadequate in some way ("I'll never amount to anything"). You might linger on images of your deceased loved one or on the look on your supervisor's face when she told you that the company is laying you off.

When you're feeling anxious, the thoughts are about future threats or dangers. These are the what-ifs of your anxious mind: "What if I fail the test and flunk out of college?" "What if I say the wrong thing and she thinks I'm weird?" Then there are the images of the car wreck or your doctor giving you bad news about your health. In chapter 6, you'll learn about the role inflexible thinking plays in your excessive and persistent anxiety or depression, along with skills to build more flexible thinking.

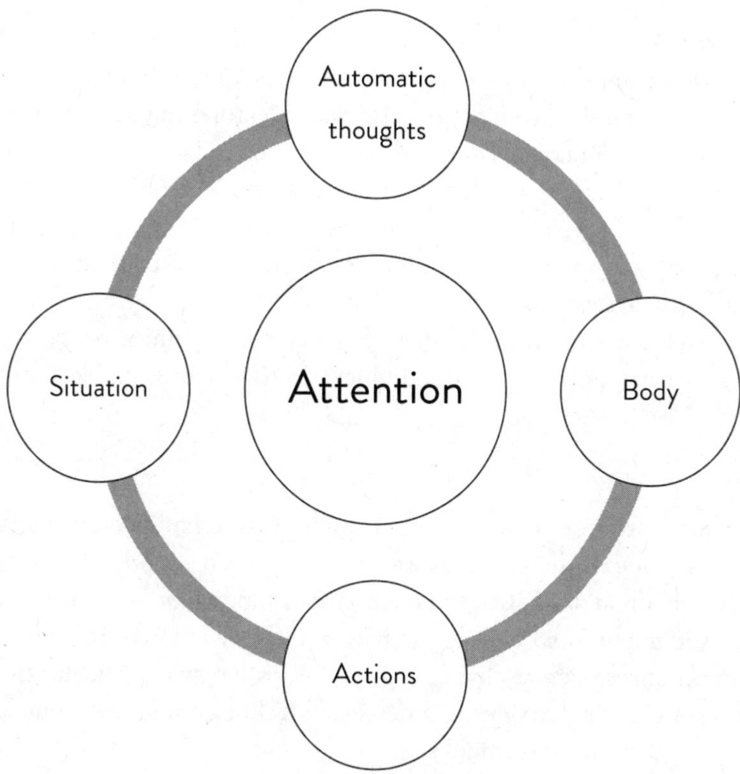

Figure 2.1. Basics of Anxiety and Depression

Physical Sensations

Your body responds physically when you feel anxious or depressed. For example, when you're anxious you might feel short of breath and your heart might race. Or your palms might sweat and you might feel nauseous and dizzy. An anxious body is better prepared to spring into action. In fact, an anxious body means that your body is shifting resources in order to enhance your performance and protect you from danger.

When you're sad or depressed, your body is heavy and slow. Your body may want more sleep, more food, or more comfort in order to process the event and grieve. Your body is not tense and ready for action but slowed and ready for inaction.

Attention

Attention is an important part of your emotional response. Your attention follows your thoughts. When you're anxious or depressed, your attention locks on features of your external or internal environment. For example, if you're home alone and hear a sound outside, your attention automatically turns toward the sound as you try to identify what it is and whether it's dangerous. Or if you're attending a party and feel depressed because your partner left you, you might focus on the couples there who appear happy and in love. You might also focus on internal features of your emotional experience, such as physical sensations, images, or actions.

In chapter 5, you'll learn about the role attention plays in maintaining your excessive anxiety and depression. You'll also learn skills, such as mindfulness, to build more flexible attention.

Action

Every emotion motivates you to act in certain ways. Nature has given you a finely tuned emotional compass to guide you in the world. These emotion-driven actions include both physical and mental actions. If you're afraid of heights, you might avoid standing on balconies or climbing ladders. If you're depressed, you might avoid pleasant activities you once enjoyed. In addition, you might try to avoid internal experiences, such as physical sensations, or suppress particular thoughts or images. Repeatedly avoiding or escaping anxious and depressed feelings diminishes your tolerance of these feelings, which causes you to avoid them all the more.

In chapter 7, you'll learn about the role of inflexible actions, such as avoidance and emotion-driven behaviors, in intensifying and maintaining your anxiety and depression. You'll also learn skills to build more flexible action.

Learning Your Emotion Basics

Now that you know the basics of emotion—thoughts, physical sensations, attention, and action—you can apply them to your own anxious or depressed feelings. Remember, you may be more aware of your physical sensations than your thoughts in some situations. Or you may be more aware of the thoughts that fuel your anxious and depressed feelings but less aware of the mental or physical actions you use to avoid or escape these feelings. And when you're feeling *intensely* anxious and depressed, it can be difficult to identify the thoughts fueling these feelings. However, with practice, you can identify all the basic parts even in the moment.

Before you start filling out the Basics of Emotion Worksheet, look at the emotion basics for Mateo and Janine. Mateo suffers with panic disorder (anxiety) and Janine suffers with major depression. See how they filled out their worksheets.

Mateo's Basics of Emotion Worksheet

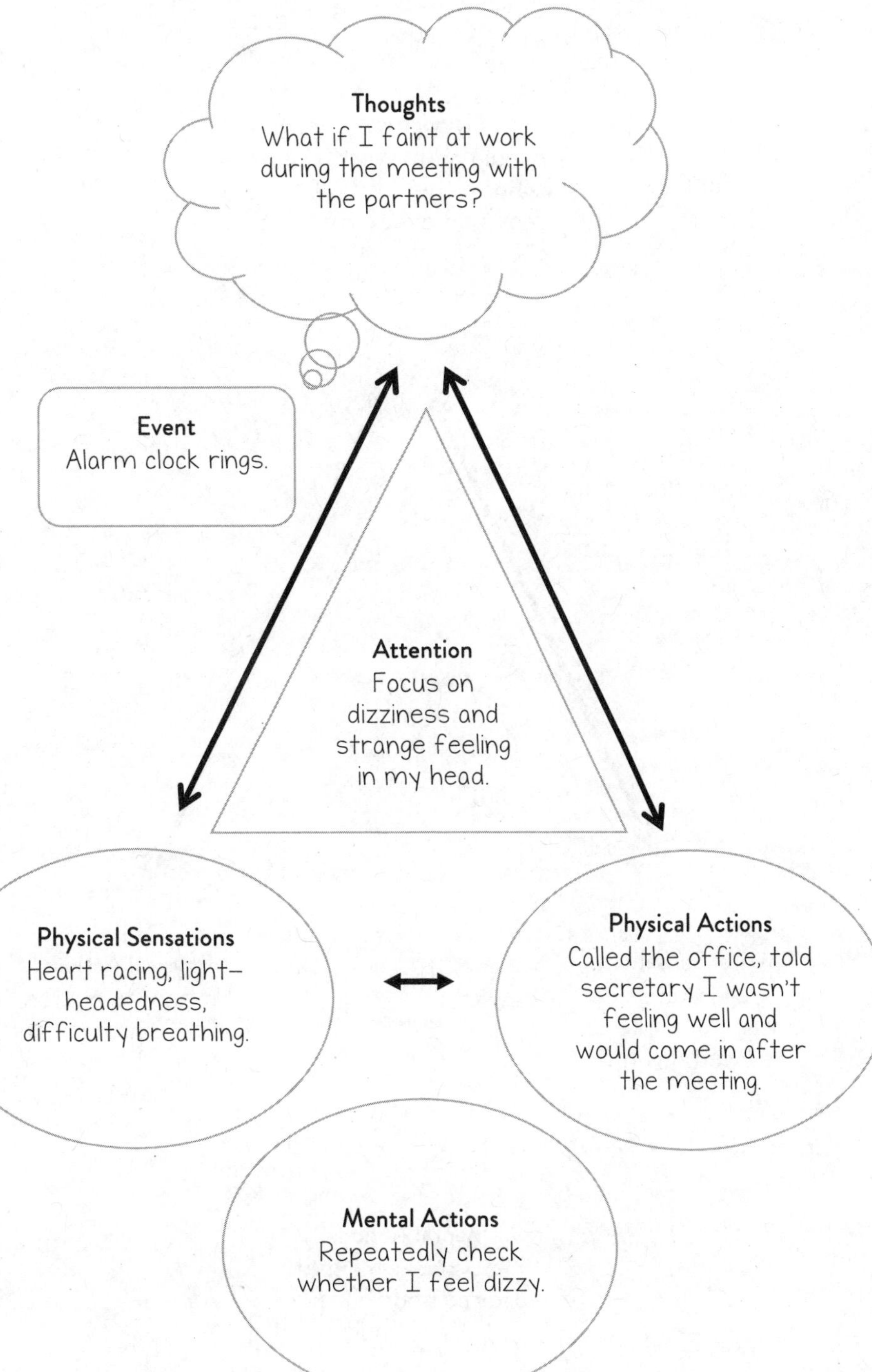

Janine's Basics of Emotion Worksheet

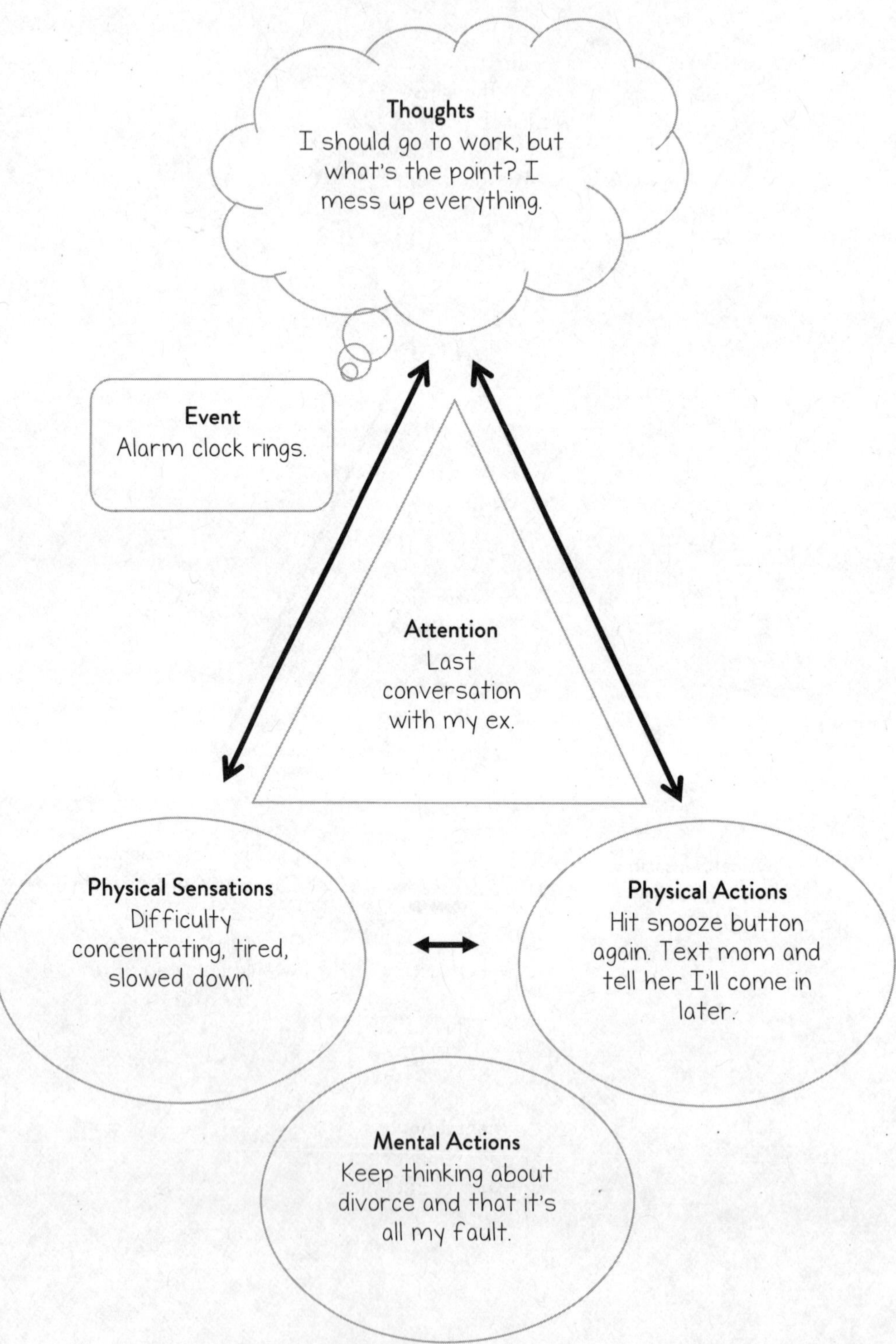

Now, complete a blank Basics of Emotion Worksheet for at least three episodes when you were feeling intensely anxious or depressed. Identify each specific event, activity, and time of day. This can help you recall what you were thinking, doing, and attending to during the episode. If you're having trouble recalling what you were thinking, close your eyes and imagine that you're back in the situation. The more times you practice this exercise the easier it becomes to identify all the basic parts of your anxious and depressed feelings.

Basics of Emotion Worksheet

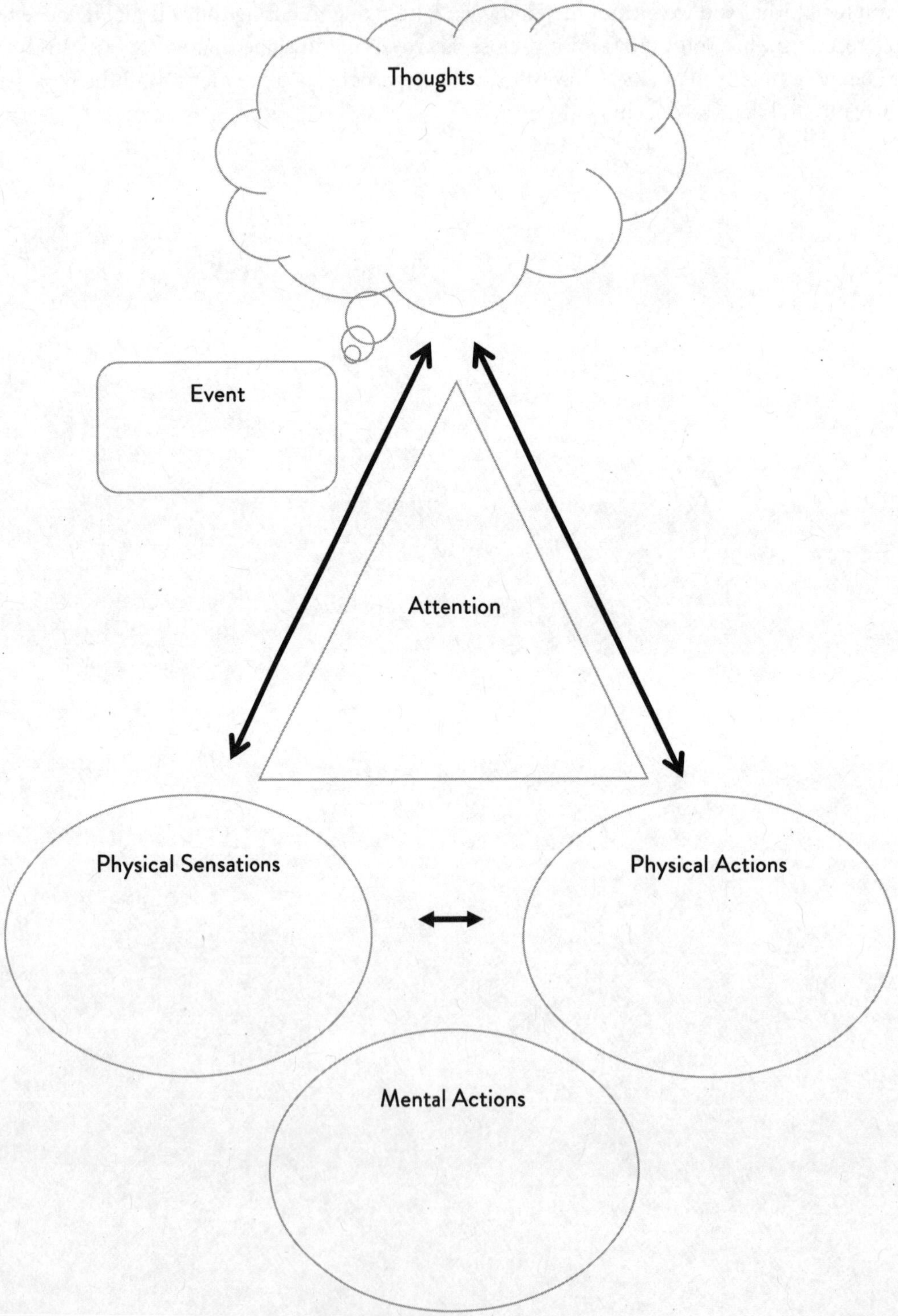

Self-Test: Depression, Anxiety, and Stress

To give you a sense of how you're doing now, complete the following simple test. It'll help you assess the current levels of your anxiety, depression, and stress. Halfway through this workbook, you'll complete this test again to check your progress. Then, at the end, you'll retake it one last time to see how far you've come. Nothing succeeds like success, and nothing builds success more than seeing that what you're learning and practicing is helping.

Depression, Anxiety, and Stress Test

Date: ________________

Instructions: Read each statement and rate how much the statement applied to you *during the past week*. These results are for educational purposes only. If you are concerned in any way about your health, please consult with a qualified professional.

Rating Scale

0: Did not apply to me at all

1: Applied to me to some degree or for some of the time

2: Applied to me to a considerable degree or for a good part of the time

3: Applied to me very much or most of the time

1.	I found myself getting upset by quite trivial things.	
2.	I was aware of dryness of my mouth.	
3.	I couldn't seem to experience any positive feelings at all.	
4.	I experienced breathing difficulty (breathlessness or excessively rapid breathing) in the absence of physical exertion.	
5.	I just couldn't seem to get going.	
6.	I tended to overreact to situations.	

7.	I had a feeling of shakiness (for example, feeling weak in the knees).	
8.	I found it difficult to relax.	
9.	I found myself in situations that made me so anxious that I was most relieved when they ended.	
10.	I felt that I had nothing to look forward to.	
11.	I found myself getting upset rather easily.	
12.	I felt that I was using a lot of nervous energy.	
13.	I felt sad and depressed.	
14.	I found myself getting impatient when I was delayed in any way (for example, in lines or at traffic lights).	
15.	I had a feeling of faintness.	
16.	I felt that I had lost interest in just about everything.	
17.	I felt I wasn't worth much as a person.	
18.	I felt that I was rather touchy.	
19.	I perspired noticeably (for example, sweaty hands) in the absence of high temperatures or physical exertion.	
20.	I felt scared without any good reason.	
21.	I felt that life wasn't worthwhile.	
22.	I found it hard to wind down.	
23.	I had difficulty in swallowing.	
24.	I couldn't seem to get any enjoyment out of the things I did.	

25.	I was aware of the action of my heart in the absence of physical exertion (for example, sensing my heart rate increase, noticing my heart missing a beat).	
26.	I felt down-hearted and blue.	
27.	I was very irritable.	
28.	I felt I was close to panic.	
29.	I found it hard to calm down after something upset me.	
30.	I feared that I would be "thrown" by some trivial but unfamiliar task.	
31.	I was unable to become enthusiastic about anything.	
32.	I found it difficult to tolerate interruptions to what I was doing.	
33.	I was in a state of nervous tension.	
34.	I felt I was pretty worthless.	
35.	I was intolerant of anything that kept me from getting on with what I was doing.	
36.	I felt terrified.	
37.	I could see nothing in the future to be hopeful about.	
38.	I felt that life was meaningless.	
39.	I found myself getting agitated.	
40.	I was worried about situations in which I might panic and make a fool of myself.	
41.	I experienced trembling (for example, in my hands).	
42.	I found it difficult to work up the initiative to do things.	

Instructions: Enter the rating you gave each question (Q). Add the two ratings in each row, then enter this value in the unshaded box. For example, if Q1 has a rating of 1 and Q22 has a rating of 2, add 1 and 2, then place the value 3 in the unshaded box for "Stress Score." Last, add the scores in each column to give you the total Depression, Anxiety, and Stress scores.

Q	Rating	Q	Rating	Depression Score	Anxiety Score	Stress Score
1.		22.				
2.		23.				
3.		24.				
4.		25.				
5.		26.				
6.		27.				
7.		28.				
8.		29.				
9.		30.				
10.		31.				
11.		32.				
12.		33.				
13.		34.				
14.		35.				

15.		36.				
16.		37.				
17.		38.				
18.		39.				
19.		40.				
20.		41.				
21.		42.				
				Total D Score:	**Total A Score:**	**Total S Score:**

	Normal	**Mild**	**Moderate**	**Severe**	**Very Severe**
Depression	0 to 9	10 to 13	14 to 20	21 to 27	28 +
Anxiety	0 to 7	8 to 9	10 to 14	15 to 19	20 +
Stress	0 to 14	15 to 18	19 to 25	26 to 33	34 +

Remember, whereas every emotion is composed of thoughts, physical sensations, particular things you pay attention to, and particular actions you take or don't take, it's the *inflexible* way you think, attend, and act that causes you to suffer. In this workbook, you'll learn skills to build your emotional flexibility and thereby suffer less.

Long Story Short

The skills in this workbook will help you recover from anxiety and depressive disorders, as well as from periods in which you feel more anxious or down than usual in response to a stressful life event. As you progress through this workbook, remember:

- Emotions, such as anxiety and depression, are normal and useful, in part because they're flexible responses to life's ups and downs. It's only when these emotional responses lose their flexibility that they become emotional disorders.
- Whether you suffer with a single anxiety disorder or several, or whether you're both anxious and depressed, the approach in this workbook can help you feel and function better.
- Emotions are composed of thoughts and images, physical sensations, attention, and physical and mental actions. It is the inflexibility of these emotional parts that contributes to excessive anxiety and depressive feelings.

Chapter 3

Record the ABCs of Emotion

Before you learned to read, you learned your ABCs. It's the same with learning to manage your anxiety and depression: before you learn to read your emotions, you must first learn the ABCs of each anxious or depressed episode. Don't worry, this alphabet is easy to learn and only contains three letters: A, B, and C.

Every emotion, including anxiety and depression, marches through this short alphabet, from the *antecedent*, the event or situation that triggers the emotion; to the *basic* thoughts, images, physical sensations, and physical and mental actions that characterize your response to that emotion; to the *consequences* of the way you respond to the emotion you felt.

Moreover, it's not enough to simply get to know your ABCs—you'll also learn how to describe them. You'll get a lot of written practice recording the ABCs of your emotions in this chapter and all chapters.

Benefits of Recording Your Emotions

There are a number of benefits to recording your emotions. First, as you record episodes of feeling anxious or depressed, you practice stepping out of these feelings—if only for a moment—to observe them rather than react to them. From this new perspective, you learn the when, where, and why of your anxious or depressed feelings, which can lessen their intensity.

Also, as you record your anxious or depressed feelings, you'll learn the factors that increase and maintain them, which can help you feel more in control of them. In fact, many people notice that just the act of recording their anxious and depressed feelings helps them feel better. In chapter 5, you'll learn additional skills to observe rather than react to your emotional experiences.

Second, as you record your anxious or depressed feelings, you'll learn that these feelings don't come out of nowhere—even if they feel like it sometimes. In fact, as you observe and then record these feelings, you'll learn that they're quite predictable. Once you learn they're predictable, you're better prepared to catch them early. Catching these emotional moments when they're small and as they arise will help you get ahead of your feelings—before they intensify and you automatically try to avoid or control them.

Third, as you become an expert on your anxious and depressed feelings, you'll learn that your interpretations of the intensity, duration, and frequency of these feelings aren't always accurate. For instance, you might think that last week was very bad, when in fact your written log of emotions shows that there were several days when you felt pretty good. This discovery can help you to feel less hopeless or overwhelmed. As you learn to record your emotional responses, you'll get a more accurate picture of what's happening in the moment. And odds are this new perspective will help you to feel more centered and better able to manage your anxious and depressed feelings.

Last, as you observe and record your anxious or depressed feelings, you'll be able to identify the emotion-driven actions that you use to avoid or escape these feelings, such as checking and rechecking your emails for errors, or seeking reassurance from your spouse that the pain you're feeling is a headache rather than a brain tumor. You'll also learn that there are costs and consequences of avoiding your anxious and depressed feelings. Understanding the consequences of your emotion-driven actions will motivate you to persist in your goal of building emotional flexibility. Greater emotional flexibility is the key to less anxiety and depression—and more freedom to do the things that matter to you.

ABCs of Anxiety and Depression

Although it may feel like it at times, your emotions don't come out of nowhere. Your anxious or depressed feelings are triggered by certain events or situations that cause you to react and act in particular ways, and these acts cost you. The more you know where your anxious and depressed feelings come from and how they affect you, the better you'll be at learning to think and act in reasonable, more flexible ways. Let's look at each of the ABCs.

A Is for Antecedents

An *antecedent* is the event that triggers the thoughts or images that are part of your anxious or depressed feelings. These events can be objects (like a barking dog if you're afraid of dogs), situations (like a test you're worried about failing), or activities (such as climbing a flight of stairs). Even thoughts, such as memories of past events, can be antecedents that trigger the thoughts that make you feel anxious or down.

At times, a physical sensation can trigger thoughts or images that influence your anxious and depressed feelings. For example, a person with a headache might think, "What if I have a brain tumor?" A person who feels anxious and light-headed while driving might think, "What if I pass out and lose control of the car?"

B Is for Basics

In the previous chapter, you learned the *basics* of your emotional response to antecedents. To recap, they consist of:

- **Thoughts and images:** These are the thoughts and images that fuel your anxious and depressed feelings. These are the what-ifs of anxiety and the "what's the point" of depression.
- **Attention:** Your attention is an important part of your emotional responses. What you pay attention to and what you ignore fuel and maintain your anxious and depressed feelings.
- **Physical sensations:** Your body responds differently to anxiety and depression. An anxious body is tense and tight. A depressed body is slow and heavy.
- **Physical and mental actions:** Physical actions are your attempts to control or dampen your anxious or depressed feelings, including avoiding situations that trigger them. Mental actions have the same goal as physical actions: to control or dampen your emotional experiences.

C Is for Consequences

Finally, the *consequences* are what happens after you escape from or avoid your emotional response. Although avoiding your anxious or depressed feelings provides you with quick short-term relief, repeatedly and automatically avoiding your anxious and depressed feelings sets you up for long-term pain.

Consequences differ for each person and for each particular episode of anxiety or depression. A consequence might be short term, such as the guilt you feel after skipping your niece's piano recital. At other times, the consequences might be long term, such as losing a job because you called in sick too often, or losing friends because you're too anxious or too down to go out with them.

These long-term consequences not only affect your life day to day, they build until each day of your life becomes harder and the scope of your life narrower. If you have a long-term pattern of avoiding your anxious and depressed feelings, then you likely have a life filled with long-term consequences.

Let's look at the four types of long-term consequences.

Emotional Consequences

People caught in a pattern of emotion-driven actions often feel sad, guilty, frustrated, or ashamed because of what they do to escape their anxious and depressed feelings. If you're late to work because you must repeatedly check that you've locked all the doors and windows in your home, you might feel frustrated with yourself and think that you're a loser.

You might feel embarrassed that you can't do things your friends do because you believe that you're too anxious or too depressed to hang out with them. You might feel ashamed by some of your thoughts and behaviors, and yet feel powerless to stop them. You might feel guilty because you believe that you're too worried or too down to attend an important function. These emotional consequences start small, but year after year the weight of these emotional consequences build until you don't like yourself or your life much.

Relationship and Family Consequences

Emotion-driven actions can damage once-loving and caring relationships. Your friends and family might have been patient with your tendency to avoid events or activities at first. They might have said, "Oh, well, that's just the way Marcie is." But over time, they've become less patient and less forgiving of your absences and excuses. After a time, your friends might call you less often, either because they know that you'll say no or because they're angry with your continued reluctance to try things that trigger your anxious or depressed feelings.

Your partner might feel burdened that you're overly dependent or may be tired of making excuses for you to loved ones when you're feeling anxious or down. Your children might feel disappointed because you don't attend their ballgames or school performances. Those who care about you might have resigned themselves to having a half of a parent, half of a spouse, or half of a friend. Even if they don't tell you that they're angry or disappointed, you can feel it, which makes you feel even more anxious, down, and deeply disappointed with yourself.

Work and Professional Consequences

Emotion-driven actions can cause long-term consequences in your work and professional life. If you're too anxious to be assertive, you might find that you don't advance as quickly as your colleagues do, even though you're as capable and hardworking as they are. Your boss might pass you over for a promotion because you're chronically late to work. You may feel too anxious or down to advocate for yourself or to take on new opportunities at work.

Health Consequences

Emotion-driven actions can have long-term consequences on your health too. You might skip meals or eat fast food because you're worried that you'll miss a deadline. You may binge on ice cream and cookies when you're feeling down, and now your back and legs hurt because you've gained weight. You might have started to drink a glass or two of wine at night to unwind, but the alcohol has worsened your sleep, anxiety, and depression—and you can't seem to cut back.

Perhaps the biggest consequence of emotion-driven actions is that they prevent you from learning something that would help you feel less anxious or depressed in the future: that you can tolerate these feelings without using emotion-driven actions.

Andy and Abby's ABCs of Emotion

Andy struggles with anxiety and Abby struggles with depression. Both are overwhelmed by their intense emotional experiences and both don't understand why they feel the way they do. Let's read about their situations and then look at how each of them filled out their ABCs of Emotion Worksheet.

The alarm clock rings. Andy thinks, "What if I can't find another job?" He knows that he won't go back to sleep. He's too tense and his mind is racing. Andy throws back the covers, stands, and shakes his head back and forth, trying to stop worrying.

He walks to the kitchen. He's nauseous but forces himself to eat a slice of toast and drink a cup of tea. As he eats, he thinks about the meeting with his boss two months ago. That's when his boss told him that he and several other people in the company had been laid off. His boss reassured Andy that it wasn't about his performance and that he'd happily write Andy a letter of recommendation to find a new job.

Since then, Andy has been worrying nonstop but not doing much to find another job. He keeps reworking his résumé but doesn't send it out. He's thinking about calling several former colleagues for lunch to network, but he's avoiding calling them. He worries about what they'll think about him now that he's unemployed. Andy is frustrated with himself because he knows what to do but he's avoiding doing it. He keeps telling himself he should work to find a new job, but he's paralyzed.

Andy's ABCs of Emotion Worksheet

Antecedent	Basics of Emotion				Consequences
	Thoughts	Attention	Physical Sensations	Actions	
The alarm clock rings.	What if I don't find another job? What if people think I'm a loser because I lost my job?	My memory of the meeting with my boss. Mistakes I've made at work over the years.	Tense. Mind racing. Nausea. Trouble sitting still.	Avoid working on résumé or networking with people.	No job. More job worry because I'm not looking for a job.

The alarm clock rings. Abby thinks, "What's the point? I'll never find another job." She knows that she won't go back to sleep although she's exhausted. Slowly, she pushes back the covers and sits on the edge of the bed with her head in her hands.

Abby forces herself to stand up and slowly walks to the kitchen. She used to enjoy breakfast. She'd sip her tea while she watched the birds at the feeder. Now she doesn't even make tea. She also used to enjoy socializing, but Abby hasn't gone out with friends in weeks. When they call, she doesn't pick up, and then feels guilty about ignoring them.

She forces herself to eat a piece of bread. Abby doesn't have the energy to toast it. As she chews, the face of her boss flashes in her mind, and she replays when he told her about the layoff. Her boss reassured her that she was a terrific employee and that he'd happily write her a letter of recommendation. But Abby's too overwhelmed to even look at her résumé, much less rework it. She thinks, "How could I have been so stupid to do that?" as she goes over and over in her mind every decision she's made in her career. She tells herself that she's a loser and that her boss was just being kind. She's convinced no one will ever hire her.

Abby's ABCs of Emotion Worksheet

Antecedent	Basics of Emotion				Consequences
	Thoughts	Attention	Physical Sensations	Actions	
The alarm clock rings.	My memory of the meeting with my boss..	What's the point? I'll never find another job because I'm stupid and a loser. What I didn't accomplish at work over the years.	Sluggish. Trouble concentrating. No appetite. No feeling of joy.	Avoid working on my résumé or networking with people.	No job. Might lose friends. Feel guilty that I'm not calling friends back.

As you can tell from their worksheets, Andy and Abby's ABCs are similar in some ways and different in others.

When it comes to the *antecedent* for their episodes of anxiety and depression, though Andy and Abby are struggling with different feelings, they share the same trigger of their emotional response: the alarm clock rings.

In terms of the *basics*, both Andy and Abby are experiencing the thoughts and mental images that characterize their anxiety and depression. They're paying attention to the aspects of their respective situations that support their feelings of anxiety and depression, while ignoring the things that don't. And they're acting in an effort to decrease the anxiety and depression they feel, when they're actually triggering more anxious and depressed feelings.

For example, Andy avoids working on his résumé because he's anxious that he might not find another job. Abby avoids the same task because she's depressed and believes that there's no point in trying to find a new job, since no one will hire her because she's stupid and a loser. Regardless of Andy and Abby's reasons, their emotions are driving their unhelpful actions.

Finally, when it comes to the *consequences* of their emotion-driven actions, the longer that Andy puts off working on his résumé or networking with colleagues, the longer it will take him to find a job. And the longer Abby avoids connecting with friends, the more likely it'll be that she'll lose them.

Rosario, Mateo, and Janine's ABCs of Emotion

Before you begin to record your own ABCs of emotion, it's helpful to look at a few more examples to familiarize yourself with the steps. Let's see how Rosario, Mateo, and Janine (review their stories in chapter 1) completed their worksheets.

Remember Rosario? She's the teacher with social anxiety disorder who worries about speaking in front of her class, particularly when she feels like she's blushing.

Rosario is the teacher representative to the school's PTA, and she's in the school conference room with other members of the committee. Rosario is speaking with parents when she begins to worry that she's started to blush. Her face and neck feel warm. She can't get out of her mind that she's beet red. She's thinking that the principal and parents are wondering what's going on with her. Rosario feels nauseous and her heart is racing. As she looks around the room, she's convinced that everyone thinks she's weird.

She manages to get through the meeting but leaves early and calls in sick the next day. All day long and for the next few days, she's upset with herself. Rosario's certain she made a fool of herself and tells her principal that she no longer wants to serve as the teacher representative for the school's PTA committee. In addition, she tells the principal that she's thinking about making this her final year of teaching.

Rosario's ABCs of Emotion

Date: May 24					
Antecedent	**Basics of Emotion**				**Consequences**
	Thoughts	**Attention**	**Physical Sensations**	**Actions**	
Attending PTA committee meeting.	What if I blush in front of the principal? He'll think I'm weird.	Warm feeling on face and neck.	Face and neck feel warm. Nauseous. Heart racing.	Leave meeting early. Call in sick next day.	Upset with myself because I left meeting. Miss professional opportunity. Told principal I might quit teaching, which upset him.

Next, look at Mateo's worksheet. Remember Mateo? He's the attorney with panic disorder. He's terrified when he feels dizzy or light-headed.

Mateo is attending a networking event of the local chapter of the American Bar Association. He is chatting with the senior partner of his firm and other attorneys in a conference room at the hotel. As Mateo looks around the room, he begins to feel intensely dizzy. He steps back to lean against a table, convinced that he might pass out at any moment. His heart is beating furiously and he's sweating and feeling short of breath. Mateo tells the group that he's going to the restroom and quickly leaves.

He calls his wife to pick him up. All that night Mateo worries what his other colleagues are thinking about his hasty retreat. He's feeling guilty that he's letting down the firm. He's certain that his days at the firm are numbered and calls in sick for the next three days. He refuses to return calls from the senior partner, who is simply checking in on how Mateo is feeling.

Mateo's ABCs of Emotion

Date: March 13

Antecedent	Basics of Emotion				Consequences
	Thoughts	Attention	Physical Sensations	Actions	
Attending event with senior partner.	What if I feel dizzy and panic?	Dizzy feeling.	Intense dizziness. Heart racing. Sweating.	Lean against table. Leave event. Don't return calls from senior partner.	Worry all night that my career is over. Feel guilty that I let down the firm. Miss more days of work, more worry.

Last, look at Janine's worksheet. Janine is depressed following her divorce, and she hasn't been out of the house socially in weeks, until now.

Janine is attending a birthday party for a friend of her youngest child. She's standing near the snacks and can't stop eating chips and other junk food. Janine compares herself to the other parents and feels guilty that she's not chatting with them. She looks down to avoid catching their eyes. The thought of hearing about their lives, which she assumes are happier than hers, feels unbearable. Janine's thinking that she's a horrible mother and that her husband was right to leave her. She begins to feel more and more depressed.

When the host mother walks up to say hello, Janine tells her that she isn't feeling well and must leave. The host mother is kind and encourages Janine to leave her daughter, saying that she'll bring her home after the party. Janine agrees to this, but as she walks to her car she tells herself that she's a horrible mother who only cares about herself. When Janine returns home she goes to bed and binges on junk food while she waits for the other mother to bring her daughter home.

Janine's ABCs of Emotion

Date: July 7					
Antecedent	**Basics of Emotion**				**Consequences**
	Thoughts	**Attention**	**Physical Sensations**	**Actions**	
Attending a birthday party with kids and other parents.	I'm a horrible parent. My husband was right to leave me. I'm a total loser.	Look at other parents and see that I'm not like them.	Exhausted, slow, can't focus.	Binge on junk food. Stand alone and not look at other parents.	Guilty because I'm not playing with my kids. More depressed at home.

The ABCs of Rosario, Mateo, and Janine are interesting in that each share the same *antecedent*—going to a social event—yet their *basics* are different. In the case of Rosario, the important element of the antecedent was that she thought others could see that she was blushing and, because of that, thought she was weird; this caused Rosario to pay attention to blushing physical sensations.

In the case of Mateo, the important element of the antecedent was that standing triggered dizzy feelings that he feared would cause him to pass out or provoke another panic attack; this caused Mateo to focus on his dizzy feelings. For Janine, the important element of the antecedent was that the other parents were engaged with each other and their children; this caused Janine to compare herself to them and focus on their interactions. As she watched, she convinced herself that she's a horrible mother and a loser, and that it was her fault that her husband divorced her.

Record Your ABCs of Emotion

Now that you know what the ABCs of anxiety and depression mean, it's time to record your own ABCs. Recording the ABCs of your emotional responses is a skill that is vital to your recovery from excessive anxiety and depression. However, it may be difficult at first, because in order to record the ABCs of your emotional responses, you must observe them too.

It's likely that you're not accustomed to observing your emotional responses in this way—or observing them at all. As you observe and then record your emotions, rather than avoiding them, you might notice that you feel a bit more anxious or down. That's okay. With time, observing and recording gets easier, in part because you're building your tolerance to your emotions rather than repeatedly avoiding them.

To start, select a situation that's still fresh in your mind. This is the *antecedent*. Keep in mind that an antecedent can be a recent situation or a past one; it can even be a consequence from a previous anxious episode. For example, if all night long you worried about the consequences from the day before and awakened tired and out of sorts, the resulting fatigue might be the antecedent for your next anxious episode: worrying about how you'll perform at work because you're tired. Or you might remember how you left a meeting because you were feeling too down, and now the antecedent includes not only the meeting today but also the memory of how you left the meeting the week before. Regardless of the antecedent, what matters is that it triggers your particular *basics* and results in your particular *consequences*.

On the lines provided, describe the details of the situation in which you were feeling anxious or depressed. Try to be as specific as you can. The more specifically you describe the event, the better you'll be able to identify the basics (thoughts, physical sensations, attention, and actions) that the event triggered.

____

____

____

Next, describe the thoughts and images that were going through your mind before you began to feel anxious or depressed.

____

____

____

This can be difficult until you get the hang of it. If you're having trouble catching the thoughts, close your eyes and try to recall the situation and how you were feeling. Then, identify the thoughts and images that arise as you imagine the situation.

Next, describe the physical sensations you felt in your body before and while you were feeling anxious or depressed. Try to be as specific as you can. Remember, your body is part of your emotional response. If you're anxious, you might notice that you feel jittery and tense. If you're depressed, you might notice that your body feels heavy and slow.

____

____

____

Next, describe where your attention was focused. Remember, when you're anxious or depressed, your attention might focus on a physical sensation, on some feature of the event or situation, on a particular thought or image, or even on an urge or impulse. Try to be as specific as you can.

____

____

____

Last, describe your emotion-driven actions. Again, these are the physical and mental actions you use to avoid your anxious and depressed feelings, control them, or escape them. Did you cut a meeting short to avoid saying something awkward or did you avoid attending the meeting altogether? Did you reassure yourself or spend countless hours analyzing and reanalyzing an event in an effort to feel less anxious or less down?

____

____

____

Now, fill out the ABCs of Emotion Worksheet, describing the ABCs for this anxious or depressed episode.

ABCs of Emotion

Date:					
Antecedent	**Basics of Emotion**				**Consequences**
	Thoughts	**Attention**	**Physical Sensations**	**Actions**	

That's it! Now you know how to record your emotional responses with the ABCs of Emotion Worksheet. During the next week or so, use blank ABCs of Emotion Worksheets to record one or two more situations in which you're feeling anxious or depressed. Any anxious or depressed response will do. They don't have to be situations in which you felt very anxious or very down. In fact, you'll often learn as much from the situations in which your anxiety or depression is low as you will from situations in which these emotions are intense.

Furthermore, situations in which you feel a little anxious or down tend to occur more often than the situations in which these emotions run high, so you're likely to catch more situations and get more practice breaking down your emotional responses.

Long Story Short

As you record the ABCs of your anxious and depressed feelings, remember:

- Observing and recording your anxious or depressed feelings provides some perspective on your emotional responses, which can help you feel a bit less anxious or down.
- As you record your ABCs, you'll learn that you tend to think, act, and focus on the same things over and over. This inflexibility causes you to avoid these feelings, and this contributes to your emotional inflexibility.
- The particular emotion-driven actions you use to avoid or control your anxious or depressed feelings maintain your emotion avoidance. Furthermore, your tendency to avoid your feelings in this way results in short-term and long-term consequences.

Chapter 4

Build Motivation and Set Goals

People who suffer with excessive anxiety and depression often have trouble doing the things that they know would help them feel better. Change is difficult, particularly when you're anxious or depressed. In fact, the emotional inflexibility that maintains your anxious and depressed feelings is one of the primary reasons it's difficult to move forward in life, including moving forward with your recovery.

In this chapter, you'll learn how motivation is an essential ingredient in the process of recovering from your anxiety or depression. You'll start with learning about the effects emotional inflexibility can have on motivation.

Fear, Anxiety, and Motivation

Your fear and anxiety have held you back in life. And your fear and anxiety can hold you back in moving forward with your recovery, too, if you let it. For example, because you're anxious, you might worry that you'll feel worse if you change: that you'll have more panic attacks, that you'll worry more than you do now, that you'll feel more anxious at parties, not less.

In the following chart, you'll see typical thoughts people have when their anxiety dampens their motivation to change. You'll also see alternative thoughts that they have when feeling calm and confident, which increase their motivation to change.

In the blank cells, write your typical anxious thoughts about change in the first column. Then, in the second column, write alternative thoughts that might help you feel less anxious about change and therefore more willing to try.

Hopelessness, Depression, and Motivation

When you're depressed, everything is more difficult. The future seems bleak and hard, and you might begin to believe that your future is hopeless. Before you became depressed, you might have liked going to work, but now it feels nearly impossible to get out of bed in the morning, and you might question your ability to do even the smallest things. In the past, you might have enjoyed arts and crafts or time with friends. Now, perhaps you think, "What's the point?" Or you might wonder why anyone would want to be your friend in the first place.

Fearful and Anxious Mind vs. Calm and Confident Mind

Fearful and Anxious Mind	Calm and Confident Mind
What if I start to feel more anxious, not less, as I begin to face my fears?	I'll likely feel a bit more anxious in the short term, but I've faced other things that frightened me and over time I always felt better. There's no way to overcome fear but to face it. Deep down I know that.
What if more bad things start to happen because I let my guard down a little?	If this were true, more bad things would happen to people who are less anxious than me. I know this isn't true. Bad things happen to everyone whether they're on guard all the time or not.
What if I try and don't get better?	If I try, really try, I'll get better. All the research says that facing your fears makes you less fearful in general. And how will I know if I don't try? I've done difficult things before and I can do this too.

When you're depressed you might think that you can't get through a minute, much less get through life. Hopelessness and depression make it difficult to see beyond these feelings and remain hopeful that, with time and practice, you can and will feel better. However, the first step in recovering from your depression is to remind yourself that these thoughts and feelings are part of the problem called "depression." It can help to focus on how things used to be for you when you weren't depressed. Because there *was* such a time, even if it's difficult to recall.

In the following chart, you'll see typical thoughts people have when they're hopeless and depressed that dampen their motivation to change. And you'll also find their alternative thoughts when they're feeling hopeful and optimistic that increase their motivation to change.

In the blank cells, write your typical depressed thoughts along with alternative thoughts about change that might help you feel more hopeful and optimistic about change and therefore more willing to try.

Hopeless and Depressed Mind vs. Hopeful and Optimistic Mind

Hopeless and Depressed Mind	Hopeful and Optimistic Mind
What's the point of trying? I'll just fail again. I fail at everything I try. Why would this be any different?	The point of trying is to see whether I'll fail or not. I don't know whether this time will be different. And I don't always fail, although it feels like that a lot of the time. Sometimes I try and succeed, but I forget that. Perhaps I'll succeed at this if I try.
I'm overwhelmed. There's no way I can do one more thing. Everything feels too difficult.	Yes, I'm overwhelmed and everything feels too difficult, but that's the depression. It's important to start where I am, not where I was. If I take small steps I'll get there.
I can't imagine that I'll ever feel better. I try things but I never feel better.	Depression makes it hard for me to believe that I can feel better. Also, it's not true that I NEVER feel better when I try things. I do feel a little better. If I keep trying I'll feel better and better. That's how I overcome depression.

A Second Look at Consequences

Recovering from your anxiety or depression isn't easy. A second look at the *consequences* of repeatedly responding to your anxious or depressed feelings in the same ways can motivate you to make these important changes.

Rosario took a few minutes to examine the consequences of her emotion-driven actions. She learned that certain consequences of her emotion-driven actions were familiar but others, such as the worry and shame she feels when she avoids, were new to her.

Rosario's Second Look at Consequences of Emotion-Driven Actions

Emotion-Driven Actions	Emotional	Relationship or Family	Work or Professional	Health	Other
Situational (avoidance of people, places, activities, or things)	I feel ashamed when I avoid something because I'm anxious. I feel guilty because I depend too much on my husband.	If I give up teaching, we can't afford things that are fun or good for our family. My husband has to make excuses for me, which upsets him.	I can't give presentations or try new things. I can't share my ideas with more than a few people at a time.		
Somatic (avoidance of bodily sensations, such as blushing, breathlessness, increased heart rate, sexual arousal)	I feel ashamed and worried when I feel like I'm blushing.	I won't do things with my husband if I think I may blush.	I can't give presentations or try new things because I'm afraid I'll blush. I won't do social things with the teachers because I'm worried they think I'm weird.	I've started to exercise less because I'm afraid I'll blush.	I can't wear pretty bright colors because it will make my face look red.

Emotion-Driven Actions	Emotional	Relationship or Family	Work or Professional	Health	Other
Cognitive (avoidance of certain thoughts, images, or memories)	I get really upset with myself when I think I'm blushing. I feel ashamed when I think about times I blushed.				Any time someone mentions blushing or feeling embarrassed, I walk away, which is rude and awkward.
Neutralization (actions taken to neutralize anxiety or distress, such as seeking reassurance, using drugs or alcohol, checking, reasoning with yourself repeatedly, seeking a stronger emotion to cover the anxiety or fear)	I check my reflection in mirrors to see if I'm blushing, which annoys me.	I'm constantly asking my husband if I'm blushing, which frustrates him. I ask my husband or mother to speak to people for me or to do things for me, which frustrates them and makes their lives harder.	I ask the other teachers questions to see what they really think of me, but this makes me look like I don't know what I'm doing.	Overeating.	

Now it's your turn. Take a few minutes to review the ABCs of Emotion Worksheets you've completed. Place the consequences of your emotion-driven actions into each of the categories on the Second Look at Consequences of Emotion-Driven Actions. Pay attention to all the consequences, short term and long term, of your emotion-driven actions. Many short-term consequences, such as arriving late to work, can lead to long-term consequences, such as losing your job.

Second Look at Consequences of Emotion-Driven Actions

Emotion-Driven Actions	Emotional	Relationship or Family	Work or Professional	Health	Other
Situational (avoidance of people, places, activities, or things)					
Somatic (avoidance of bodily sensations, such as blushing, breathlessness, increased heart rate, sexual arousal)					
Cognitive (avoidance of certain thoughts, images, or memories)					

Emotion-Driven Actions	Emotional	Relationship or Family	Work or Professional	Health	Other
Neutralization (actions taken to neutralize anxiety or distress, such as seeking reassurance, using drugs or alcohol, checking, reasoning with yourself repeatedly, seeking a stronger emotion to cover the anxiety or fear)					

The North Star That Guides You

For centuries, travelers followed the North Star to navigate across vast lands and perilous seas toward important destinations. Your *values*, like the North Star, give direction to your life and motivate you to move forward in the face of difficult feelings and situations. Values are truths, beliefs, or understandings. Some values, such as charity or generosity, serve others. Other values, such as creativity or spirituality, most often serve our own welfare and growth. Values are not desires, wishes, or preferences, such as for sex, more money, or Indian food.

Values are also not the same as goals. Values are a course (for instance, sailing south along the California coast). Meanwhile, goals are specific destinations or points you reach along the way (San Francisco, Santa Barbara, Los Angeles, San Diego) as you move in the direction of a given value. In other words, goals are a product; values are a process. "Speaking truthfully and sensitively to colleagues" is a goal; integrity is the value that the goal serves. "Meeting yearly with my physician" is a goal; health is the value that the goal serves.

Exercise: Adrift or On Course

In this exercise, you'll experience what it feels like to live a life that is *off* course and *on* course, relative to your values. Set aside ten minutes of uninterrupted time for this exercise. Read the script and then close your eyes and imagine the scenario. After you complete the imagery portion, complete the written portion that follows.

Imagine that you're in a boat in the middle of the ocean when the engine stops. You try to restart the engine but the engine is dead. Although you take the engine apart, you can't fix it. You pick up the radio to call for help but realize that the radio doesn't work. You're adrift in the ocean. Nothing but ocean as far as you can see. You hope that a passing boat will rescue you, but you don't know when that might happen or even if it will happen.

As you drift up and down with each wave, you begin to think about people back home. Your family, friends, and coworkers. You think of people you know and of people who know you. They will learn that you disappeared at sea and assume that you're dead. They will come together and cry. They'll remember you and your life. They'll share their memories of you and the qualities they remember about you and the influence you had on them.

Imagine now that you're listening to these conversations unbeknownst to them. They're speaking from their hearts, and what they say is true about you. What does your life partner say about you as a person? If you have children, what do they say about you? What are the lessons about life you taught them? What do they remember about your support of them? What do your friends and coworkers say about you? What do members of your spiritual community say about you? What do people say about you as a citizen or as a neighbor? What memories do these people share about your ability to relax or have fun?

Now set a timer for five minutes as you pause and contemplate what loved ones say about you. When the alarm sounds, answer the following prompts.

Based on *the way you're living your life now*, what did the following people say about you?

Your partner: ______________________________

____

____

____

Your children: ______________________________

____

____

____

Your closest friends: ______________________________

____

____

____

Your coworkers: ______________________________

____

____

____

Your neighbors: ______________________________

____

____

____

Members of your spiritual community: ______________________________

____

____

____

Now, set the timer for another five minutes and imagine *you have lived the life you want to live.* What would you like people to say about you?

Your partner: ______________________________

____

____

____

Your children: ______________________________

____

____

____

Your closest friends: ______________________________

____

____

____

Your coworkers: ______________________________

____

____

____

Your neighbors: ____

____

____

____

Members of your spiritual community: ______________________________

____

____

____

Locate Your North Star

Your values are your North Star. Identifying values is a process of reflection and discovery. Few of us take the time to identify what is truly important to us—but when we do, we're rewarded. Your values inspire you, motivate you, nurture you, and give meaning to your life. They direct you in life and represent what you want your life to be about in a deep and personal way.

In addition, your values motivate deep change, such as breaking free from anxiety and depression. Values also help you see beyond the anxious or depressed moments that prevent you from doing what you really want to do, doing what you would do if you weren't avoiding these feelings.

Value Domains

There are ten core value domains that motivate us to strive, change, and persist. These domains cover common areas of life for most people. You'll find that some of the following value domains are very important to you and others less so; that's totally okay. Take your time as you read about each domain and ponder the questions. After each domain you'll be asked to consider your actions in accordance to the values. Don't rush through these prompts, because the greater care you take in responding, the more accurate a picture you'll get when you map out your values in the next exercise.

Health and Self-Care

This domain is about taking care of your physical health. Through this value, you connect with the life force in us all. Through this value, you get the most out of each day and each task. Terms for values in the domain of health and self-care are "health," "strength," and "vitality." Because of your anxiety or depression, do you avoid routine medical or dental care? Does your anxiety or depression cause you to avoid joining a gym or health club? Does your anxiety or depression cause you to eat too much or too little?

To get a sense of where you are and where you want to be, think through your actions over the last few weeks, then write examples of your actions.

Actions that are consistent with the health and self-care value:

____

____

____

Actions that are inconsistent with the health and self-care value:

____

____

____

On the North Star Map, which you'll see later in this chapter, place an **X** to indicate how close your actions are relative to the North Star for the health and self-care value.

Family

This domain is about the importance of your relationships with your immediate family, including you father, mother, and siblings. Through this value, you learn to love. Through this value, you find support and acceptance that stabilizes your life and acts as the springboard to loving others. Terms for values in the domain of family are "love," "acceptance," and "respect."

Does your anxiety or depression create distress or resentment in your relationships with family members? Are you overly dependent on your parents? Are you too anxious to speak your mind and, for that reason, your relationships are not as honest and truthful as you would like?

To get a sense of where you are and where you want to be, think through your actions over the last few weeks, then write examples of your actions.

Actions that are consistent with the family value:

____

____

____

Actions that are inconsistent with the family value:

____

____

____

On the North Star Map, place an **X** to indicate how close your actions are relative to the North Star for the family value.

Education and Learning

This domain is about learning and discovery. Through this value, you connect to the thrill and excitement of learning something new. Terms for values in the domain of education and learning are "truth," "wisdom," and "skill." Did you attend a college that wasn't your first choice because you were too anxious or depressed to attend a college farther away from home? Are you a life-long learner but you're too anxious or depressed to take a class? If you're a student, does your anxiety or depression prevent you from speaking to your teachers or participating fully in class discussions?

To get a sense of where you are and where you want to be, think through your actions over the last few weeks, then write examples of your actions.

Actions that are consistent with the education and learning value:

____

____

____

Actions that are inconsistent with the education and learning value:

____

____

____

On the North Star Map, place an **X** to indicate how close your actions are relative to the North Star for the education and learning value.

Community Life and Citizenship

This domain is about service to others. Through this value, you contribute to making the world better in some way. Terms for values in the domain of community life and citizenship are "justice," "responsibility," and "charity." Does your anxiety or depression keep you from charitable work or political action? Because of your anxiety or depression, do you avoid serving your community or participating in the life of your neighborhood?

To get a sense of where you are and where you want to be, think through your actions over the last few weeks, then write examples of your actions.

Actions that are consistent with the community and citizenship value:

____

____

____

Actions that are inconsistent with the community and citizenship value:

____

____

____

On the North Star Map, place an **X** to indicate how close your actions are relative to the North Star for the community and citizenship value.

Intimate Relationship

This domain is about your relationship with your significant other: spouse, partner, lover, boyfriend, or girlfriend. Through this value, you deepen your capacity to give love and to accept love. Through this value, you learn to trust and honor a special person. If you aren't with someone now, you can still connect with this domain by working toward an ideal relationship with a future person. Terms for values in the domain of intimate relationship are "fidelity," "openness," and "love."

Because of your anxiety or depression, do you avoid physical intimacy with your spouse or significant other? Do you worry excessively that your partner will leave you at any moment? Are you too anxious or depressed to ask out a special person or to say yes when a special person asks you out?

To get a sense of where you are and where you want to be, think through your actions over the last few weeks, then write examples of your actions.

Actions that are consistent with the intimate relationship value:

____

____

____

Actions that are inconsistent with the intimate relationship value:

____

____

____

On the North Star Map, place an **X** to indicate how close your actions are relative to the North Star for the intimate relationship value.

Parenting

This domain is about your life as a parent. If you don't have children, you can still connect with this domain by working toward becoming a "parent" to some future child or young adult, or by thinking about how you'd want to behave toward children who are in your life. Through this value, you learn to love another without expectation that the other will return love in equal measure. Through this value, you connect to the teacher and protector in you. Through this value, you share the wisdom you've gained in living your life with meaning and integrity. Terms for values in the domain of parenting are "love," "protecting," and "teaching."

Are you too anxious or depressed to set limits with your children so that they become responsible and caring adults? Does your anxiety or depression cause you to overprotect your children and, thereby, deny them the experiences that will make them stronger and more capable? Do you want children but are too afraid or too depressed to try?

To get a sense of where you are and where you want to be, think through your actions over the last few weeks, then write examples of your actions.

Actions that are consistent with the parenting value:

____

____

____

Actions that are inconsistent with the parenting value:

____

____

____

On the North Star Map, place an **X** to indicate how close your actions are relative to the North Star for the parenting value.

Recreation and Leisure

This domain is about seeking balance between work and play. Through this value, you connect to the child in you. Through this value, you recharge and reconnect with family and friends. You learn to appreciate the quiet moments that punctuate a life and give it rhythm and meaning. Terms for values in the domain of recreation and leisure are "creativity," "fun," and "passion."

Are you too anxious or depressed to set limits with a supervisor that keeps giving you work? Does your anxiety or depression wear you down so that you don't have the energy to have fun with a sport or activity? Does anxiety or depression keep you from pursuing leisure activities that might enrich your life?

To get a sense of where you are and where you want to be, think through your actions over the last few weeks, then write examples of your actions.

Actions that are consistent with the recreation and leisure value:

____

____

____

Actions that are inconsistent with the recreation and leisure value:

____

____

____

On the North Star Map, place an **X** to indicate how close your actions are relative to the North Star for the recreation and leisure value.

Social Life and Friendship

This domain is about the importance of friendships and having a full and vibrant social life. Through this value, you build a supportive friendship network. Through this value, you nurture caring and loyal friends. Through this value, you live fully as a social being. Terms for values in the domain of social life and friendship are "love," "loyalty," and "trust."

Does your anxiety or depression cause you to spend too much time alone? Do you decline invitations from friends to go out together because you're too depressed or anxious? Are your "friends" people who treat you poorly, but you're too anxious or too depressed to find new ones?

To get a sense of where you are and where you want to be, think through your actions over the last few weeks, then write examples of your actions.

Actions that are consistent with the social life and friendship value:

____

____

____

Actions that are inconsistent with the social life and friendship value:

____

____

____

On the North Star Map, place an **X** to indicate how close your actions are relative to the North Star for the social life and friendship value.

Spirituality and Faith

This domain is about connecting to something larger than yourself. Through this value, you learn the importance of believing in something you can't see or touch. Through this value, you connect with the arc of life—its beginning and its end. Spirituality takes many forms. For one person, spirituality might mean that you attend services of an organized religion. For another, spirituality might mean that you meditate or take long walks in the woods alone to connect with nature or to collect your thoughts. Terms for values in the domain of spirituality and faith are "God," "faith," "a higher power," and "the universe."

Does your anxiety or depression make it difficult for you to find the inner peace that means spirituality to you? Are you too fearful or depressed to attend services at your church, mosque, or temple? Do you worry so much about what your priest, rabbi, or other faith leader might think about you that you don't seek their wisdom and advice?

To get a sense of where you are and where you want to be, think through your actions over the last few weeks, then write examples of your actions.

Actions that are consistent with the spirituality and faith value:

____

____

____

Actions that are inconsistent with the spirituality and faith value:

____

____

____

On the North Star Map, place an **X** to indicate how close your actions are relative to the North Star for the spirituality and faith value.

Work and Career

This domain is about bringing integrity, passion, and excellence to your work life. Through this value, you take on new professional challenges that excite you and move your career ahead. Through this value, you earn the respect of your supervisors and coworkers. Through this value, you learn the importance of working hard for something that you believe will make a positive difference for you and others. Terms for values in the domain of work and career are "excellence," "stewardship," and "professionalism."

Are you too afraid or too depressed to take on new challenges at work? Are you so worried that your boss will fire you or that your coworkers will dislike you that you don't speak your mind? Are you too anxious or too depressed to take advantage of the opportunities that attracted you to the job in the first place?

To get a sense of where you are and where you want to be, think through your actions over the last few weeks, then write examples of your actions. Then, on the North Star Map, place an X to indicate how close your actions are relative to the North Star for the work and career value.

Actions that are consistent with the work and career value:

____

____

____

Actions that are inconsistent with the work and career value:

____

____

____

North Star Map

Place an **X** in each value domain column relative to how close your actions and activities are to the North Star for that value. If your actions are 100 percent on course and consistent with the value, you'll place the **X** in the block for the value domain closest to the North Star. The farther away the **X** is relative to the North Star, the farther your actions are off course from the value.

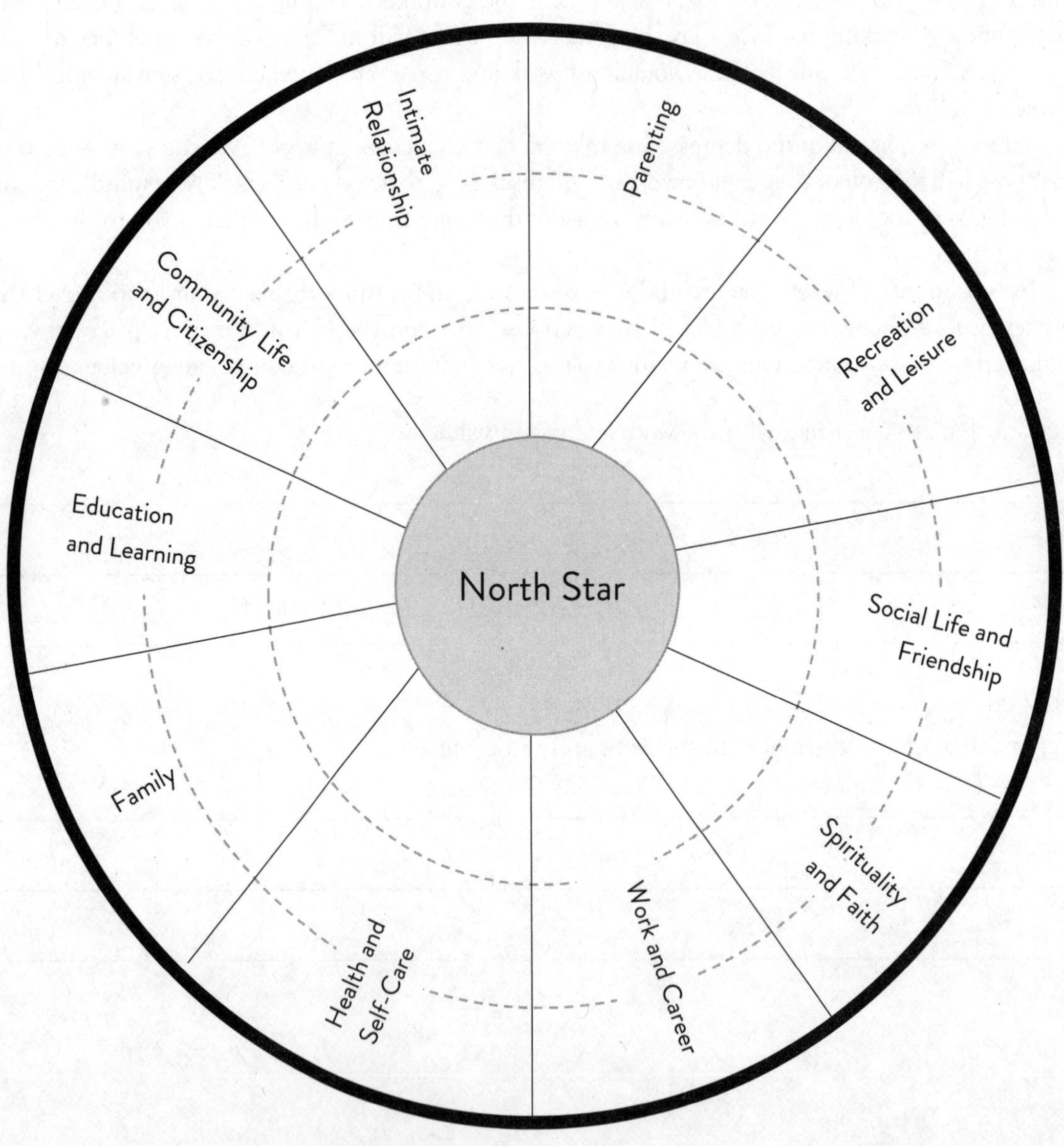

What does the map tell you? Well, the farther away your actions are from the North Star for a value, the greater the distance you are from living your life according to that value. For example, if you consistently avoid meeting with friends because you feel too anxious or down, yet social life and friendship are important to you, then your actions are inconsistent with this value. The farther away your actions are from the values that are important to you, the less likely your life is meaningful and the less likely you are to feel fulfilled and happy.

A Second Look at Your Values

Now that you've considered your actions relative to your values, you'll spend several more minutes clarifying the values that truly matter to you and that consistently direct your life. You'll use a Values Clarification Worksheet to guide you through this process. But before you begin, look at Janine's Values Clarification Worksheet. Remember Janine? She's recently divorced and very depressed. She's always wanted to be a stay-at-home mom. However, her depression is making it difficult for her to be the parent she wants to be to her kids. She's avoiding her friends and bingeing on junk food, which only make her feel worse about herself. Furthermore, Janine is missing so much work from her family's business that her parents are feeling financial stress. It's important that Janine connect to her values to move ahead in her recovery.

Janine's Values Clarification Worksheet

Domain	Value	Very Important	Somewhat Important	Not At All Important
Community life and citizenship				X
Education and learning				X
Family	Love, support	X		
Social life and friendship	Fun, support	X		
Health and self-care	Energy, strength		X	
Intimate relationship	Love, support	X		
Parenting		X		
Recreation and leisure	Balance, fun		X	
Spirituality and faith				X
Work and career				X

Now it's your turn to complete a Values Clarification Worksheet. Consider each domain carefully and think how important or unimportant it is to you. Place an **X** in the appropriate column ("Very Important," "Somewhat Important," "Not At All Important").

Values Clarification Worksheet

Domain	Value	Very Important	Somewhat Important	Not At All Important
Community life and citizenship				
Education and learning				
Family				
Social life and friendship				
Health and self-care				
Intimate relationship				
Parenting				
Recreation and leisure				
Spirituality and faith				
Work and career				

What did you learn? Did you discover values that were more important to you than you thought? Did you discover a value that consumes much of your action and attention but that's not particularly important to you?

____

____

____

____

Follow Your North Star

Following your North Star means that you make a commitment to feel anxious or depressed in the service of your values. Committing to act according to your values creates willingness on your part, and willingness leads to action. Through willingness, you gain some influence over how you feel and what you do—and you make what seems unbearable a bit more bearable. And through willingness and committed action in the service of your values, you take control of your recovery.

Track Your Current Course

Tracking what you do relative to what you would like to do is a simple way to increase your awareness of the ways that your anxious and depressed feelings take you off course. You'll use the My Values-Driven Actions Log to do this.

In the first column, write two or three value domains that you identified as the most important to you from your Values Clarification Worksheet. In the second column, write your intentions: what you'd be doing that is 100 percent on course relative to the value if you weren't feeling anxious and depressed. Then, in the third and fourth columns, write the feelings (anxiety, depression, anger, guilt) and thoughts ("What's the point," "I can't do this," "I'm too overwhelmed") that get in the way of you acting on your intention. In the Actions column, write what you did that was inconsistent with your intentions. In the final column, each day rate the degree that you're on course relative to the value. If you're 100 percent on course, your Actions exactly match your Intentions. To understand how to do this, look at Janine's completed My Values-Driven Actions Log.

Janine's My Values-Driven Actions Log

					Degree on Course (0–100%)						
Most Important Value Domains	**Intentions** (specific behaviors; who, what, when, where)	**Thoughts**	**Feelings**	**Actions**	**Sun**	**Mon**	**Tue**	**Wed**	**Thu**	**Fri**	**Sat**
Parenting	Play board game with kids'.	I won't enjoy myself.	Depressed, exhausted.	Make excuse, sleep on couch.	50%	100%	90%	70%	90%	70%	90%
	Go to kid's soccer practices and games.	What if someone asks about my ex?	Anxious, guilty.	Ask my sister to take kids.	60%	80%	50%	100%	100%	50%	50%
Social life and friendship	Attend scrapbooking monthly meeting.	They're disappointed in me.	Anxious, guilty.	Don't go or leave early.	0%	100%	0%	0%	100%	0%	0%
	Invite Cheryl and Bonnie for girls' night out.	I should keep in touch. I'm such a loser.	Guilty, depressed.	Don't call, don't go if they invite me.	0%	100%	0%	100%	0%	0%	0%
Health and self-care	Take walk at lunch.	What's the point? I'm fat.	Exhausted, depressed.	Skip walk.	80%	80%	90%	100%	100%	80%	90%
	Snack on carrots at night.	No one cares if I'm healthy.	Depressed, angry.	Grab chips and binge.	50%	70%	70%	90%	70%	70%	80%

My Values-Driven Actions Log

					Degree on Course (0–100%)						
Most Important Value Domains	Intentions (specific behaviors; who, what, when, where)	Thoughts	Feelings	Actions	Sun	Mon	Tue	Wed	Thu	Fri	Sat

After you have completed the My Values-Driven Actions Log, describe the thoughts and images that made it difficult for you to follow through with your intention to act according to the value:

____

____

____

Describe the feelings (anxiety, depression, guilt, shame) and physical sensations (heart racing, sweating, confusion) that made it difficult for you to follow through with your intention to act according to the value:

____

____

____

Describe the actions you took to avoid, escape, or minimize your anxious depressed feelings that made it difficult for you to follow through with your intention to act according to the value:

____

____

____

Chart Your New Values-Driven Course

Now that you understand how your emotion-driven actions make it difficult for you to live a life according to the values that are deeply important to you, it's time to use these values to chart the course you'll take over the next weeks and months. In other words, the next step is to translate your values into action—building willingness, in the process, to feel what comes up as you undertake these actions.

Ultimately, your recovery depends on having both meaningful goals that are in the service of your values, as well as a clear plan to achieve those goals. A goal is not the same as a plan. The goal is the destination you hope to reach; the plan is the set of distinct steps you'll take to reach the goal. Most important, your recovery depends on your willingness to change your behaviors or actions—and connecting your actions to your values will help you do this.

To chart your values-driven course, use the following steps:

1. **Select an important values domain.** For example, Rosario selected social life and friendship. Rosario has a few close friends but she would like others, and her social anxiety has made it difficult for her to make friends and maintain the friendships she has. Janine selected parenting as the value domain most important to her. Her depression has made it difficult for her to be the parent she wants to be to her children.

2. **Translate the value into several value statements.** Value statements are short sentences or phrases that capture the value. Value statements are a bit like a motto that you wish to live by. Ask yourself, "What do I want to stand for when it comes to family? If I overheard people talking about what they admire about me, what words would I want to hear?" For example, Rosario's life motto is "I want to be a caring and supportive friend." Janine's motto is "I want to be a loving, kind, and responsible parent to my children." Here are other value statement examples for each domain:

    - Community life and citizenship: "I want to improve the lives of people who are less fortunate than myself."
    - Education and learning: "I want to be well educated and pass on my knowledge and wisdom to other people."
    - Family: "I want to build a caring and supportive family and be there for them during difficult times."
    - Health and self-care: "I want to promote my physical and mental health over my lifetime."
    - Intimate relationship: "I want to be a caring, loving, and supportive life partner."
    - Parenting: "I want to be a kind, loving, and responsible parent to my children."
    - Recreation and leisure: "I want to enjoy the beauty of nature."
    - Social life and friendship: "I want to be there for the people I care about when they need my support and time."
    - Spirituality and faith: "I want to be a spiritual person who honors and respects the spirituality of other people."
    - Work and career: "I want to continually challenge and improve myself as a person."

3. **Identify a series of specific actions that move you in the direction of your value or goal.** Make the steps small and realistic. Ask yourself, "What would I be doing or not doing?" Consider when you'd do the action, where, and with whom. Try to be as specific and concrete as possible. For example, "Invite Marsha to see a movie with me this Saturday."

Use the Chart My Values-Driven Course Worksheet to put all the steps together. To get an idea of how to do this, look at the values-driven worksheets that Rosario and Janine created.

Rosario's My Values-Driven Action Plan

1. Select the most important value domain: Education and learning.
2. Write one or more value statements: I want to educate children who will one day be citizens and leaders. I want to learn as much as I can to become the best teacher I can be.
3. Write a series of specific committed actions:

Committed action 1: Build connections to parents.

Committed action 2: Strengthen connections to teachers I know well.

Committed action 3: Build a solid relationship with the principal.

Committed action 4: Build connections with other teachers in the community.

In the service of the value: Education and learning.

I choose to feel: Anxious and uncomfortable.

So that I can: Become the best teacher I can be.

In these steps:

1. Speak to two parents at the next PTA meeting.
2. Call 5th-grade teacher and invite her to co-teach a class.
3. Chat with principal for 10 minutes at least once a week.
4. Make small talk with teachers I don't know well.

Janine's My Values-Driven Action Plan

1. Select the most important value domain: Parenting.
2. Write one or more value statements: I want to be a caring and loving parent to my children. I want to teach my children the power of perseverance.
3. Write a series of specific committed actions:

   Committed action 1: Spend quality time with my children.

   Committed action 2: Do something fun and interesting with my children.

   Committed action 3: Build connections with other parents.

   Committed action 4: Participate in my children's lives in and out of school.

   In the service of the value: Parenting.

   I choose to feel: Energized and upbeat.

   So that I can: Parent my children to the best of my abilities.

   In these steps:

   1. Every night after dinner play board game with kids.
   2. On Saturday take kids to the zoo.
   3. Call Ms. Kirk to ask if I can volunteer in Amy's class on Tuesday mornings.
   4. Invite mother of Jessica's best friend to lunch next week.

My Values-Driven Action Plan

1. Select the most important value domain: ______________________________

2. Write one or two value statements: ______________________________

____

____

____

____

3. Write a series of specific committed actions:

Committed action 1: ______________________________

____

Committed action 2: ______________________________

____

Committed action 3: ______________________________

____

Committed action 4: ______________________________

____

In the service of the value: ______________________________

____

I choose to feel: ______________________________

So that I can: ______________________________

____

In these steps:

1. ____

____

2. ____

____

3. ____

____

4. ____

____

Long Story Short

Forty years of research support the effectiveness of the approach and skills in this workbook. At the same time, the first word in the word "workbook" is "work," and it can be difficult work. Building emotional flexibility isn't easy, particularly when it comes to approaching rather than avoiding your anxious and depressed feelings. Drinking frequently from the well of motivation is essential if you are to persevere. As you progress through this workbook, remember:

- Fear and hopelessness are barriers to recovering from your anxious and depressed feelings. Remind yourself that the skills in this workbook will decrease these feelings.
- Anxiety and depression have taken your life off course. In order to get it back on course, it's essential that you follow the North Star of your values.
- Committing to act in the face of your anxious and depressed feelings will open your life and connect you to the deep and personal reasons that make life worth living.

Part II

Learn Skills to Build Your Emotional Flexibility

Chapter 5

Build Flexible Attention

As you've learned, approaching rather than avoiding your emotions enhances your emotional flexibility. But how do you that? What do you have to do to face your uncomfortable feelings? In the chapters that follow, you'll learn exactly how to build emotional resiliency. And it starts with building *flexible attention*. Flexible attention means that you can shift your attention away from the repeated thoughts, physical sensations, and actions that contribute to your persistent anxiety and depression.

To build flexible attention, you'll learn the powerful skill of *mindfulness*. Mindfulness is present-focused, nonjudgmental awareness. In this chapter, you'll try several mindfulness exercises, including ways to integrate mindfulness into daily life, that build your capacity to shift your attention from the future (home to excessive anxiety), or from the past (home to hopelessness and depression), in order to live your life in the present moment.

Mindfulness

Mindfulness is noticing and paying attention to thoughts, feelings, behavior, and everything else that's going on inside and outside you. Mindfulness includes two key characteristics:

- **Mindfulness is nonjudgmental.** When you're mindful, your intention is to observe without interpreting, evaluating, or criticizing.
- **Mindfulness is focused on the present moment.** When you're mindful, your intention is to see, hear, and feel what's happening now, rather than what might happen in the future or what might have happened in the past.

Mindfulness builds emotional flexibility in two ways:

1. **Mindfulness counters your mind's tendency to dwell or ruminate on the future or the past.** Mindfulness is rooted in the present moment, and the present moment is incompatible with what could happen or what might have happened. Now, you're likely already observing your anxious or depressed feelings. In fact, you likely have trouble observing much of anything else. However, you're likely observing *what feels true* rather than observing *what is true.*

Observing what feels true means that you pay attention—and perhaps too much attention—to how bad or overwhelmed you feel. It may feel true that life is hopeless. It may feel true that your anxiety or panic will never go away. It may feel true that your emotions are unbearable. You've likely observed your emotional responses in this way for years.

However, just because it feels true doesn't mean that it is true, and interpreting your emotions in this way only intensifies them. Ultimately, observing what is true means standing outside your emotional responses to see the present, past, and yourself the way they truly are—which can open space for you to think and act differently, and ultimately feel less intensely anxious or depressed.

2. **Mindfulness encourages you to approach rather than avoid your anxious and depressed feelings.** Mindfulness will help you resist the urges to avoid, to escape from, or to control what you're feeling—all of the emotion-driven actions that create so many problems for you. Similarly, as you learn to observe mindfully, you'll learn an alternative to suppressing or distracting yourself from your emotional responses. These too contribute to the emotional avoidance that maintains your excessive anxious and depressed feelings. In chapter 8, you'll learn all the steps involved in approaching emotions in this way. For now, explore the power of mindfulness in order to free yourself from the trap of inflexible attention.

Welcome to the Present Moment

Learning to be mindfully aware of the present moment doesn't come naturally to us. Our minds don't work that way. Our minds, by nature, take us into the future or back into the past. And this natural tendency is generally helpful. Our mind's ability to anticipate problems or threats protects us from the real dangers and difficulties we face in our lives. It also helps us learn what worked or didn't work so that we can be more effective and prepared in the future.

However, an inflexible mind that cannot shift from the future or the past easily—a mind that habitually swings out of the present moment to dwell on what feels true rather than what is true in the future or in the past—is a mind filled with suffering. Mindfulness works against your mind's natural tendency to move away from the present, so be patient. With some practice you can learn to bring it back.

Exercise: Inside and Outside

This exercise is a great introduction to mindfulness because you learn to distinguish between *inside* experiences that arise in your mind and body, and *outside* experiences that arise in the world around you.

1. Close your eyes and take a deep breath, then slowly exhale. Gently move your attention to your body. Observe any pleasant sensations or feelings. If you notice pain or tension, observe that too

but don't linger there. Perhaps you notice other sensations: heat, cold, or pressure on a part of your body. Notice the feeling of the floor beneath your feet if you're sitting, or the feeling of the bed or floor if you're lying down. Breathe normally while you observe your breath—the gentle rise and fall of your abdomen or the movement of air in and out of your nostrils.

2. After a minute or two of looking inside, open your eyes and shift your attention to the environment around you. What do you see, hear, and smell? What do you feel around you? Perhaps the texture and weight of the clothing on you, or the temperature of the air on your skin? Just move from one sense to another—sight, sound, smell, taste, and touch. Let your attention drift to sounds—the soft ticking of a clock or the hum of the air conditioner. Let your attention focus on colors and shapes around you—the pattern in the carpet or the shape of a doorknob. Let your attention wander outside the room or building to notice other sounds—a honking car horn or the sound of a door opening or closing.

3. After a minute or two of looking outside, close your eyes and shift your attention back to the inside. Open your attention to other sensations throughout your body—those that you missed before—noticing what you feel. Again, if you notice anything uncomfortable or unpleasant, rest your attention there for just a moment and move on to whatever else there is to notice. After a minute or two, open your eyes and shift your attention back to the outside one more time.

Now, take a few moments to reflect on and record your experiences using the Inside and Outside Worksheet. What did you notice in your inner and outer worlds? In which world were you most comfortable and at peace? In which world is your mind most quiet? In which world was your mind most active?

Inside and Outside Worksheet

Day of Week	Inner World			Outer World	Did You Judge Your Experience?
	Mind What did you notice about your own thoughts and images?	**Body** What did you notice about your physical sensations and feelings?	**Actions** What did you notice about your behaviors?	What did you notice around you—sights, sounds, smells?	0 (not at all) to 10 (very much)
Sunday					
Monday					
Tuesday					

Wednesday					
Thursday					
Friday					
Saturday					

Nia tried this exercise for a few days and discovered that sometimes she felt relaxed and at ease, and other times she felt frustrated and anxious. Interestingly, Nia learned that she was most at ease when she observed her senses and most frustrated and anxious when she observed her thoughts.

Nia's Inside and Outside Worksheet

Day of Week	Inner World			Outer World	Did You Judge Your Experience?
	Mind What did you notice about your own thoughts and images?	**Body** What did you notice about your physical sensations and feelings?	**Actions** What did you notice about your behaviors?	What did you notice around you—sights, sounds, smells?	0 (not at all) to 10 (very much)
Sunday	I can't focus. What if I never find a job?	I feel tense, have a headache, couldn't eat much today.	Kept looking at the clock, relaxed shoulders.	I heard birds chirping outside.	5
Monday	I noticed what-ifs. What if he leaves me? What if he doesn't love me?	More tension, especially around my eyes.	Changed position.	I listened to boyfriend humming a song.	3
Tuesday	I noticed my "put down" thoughts.	Tense, restless.	Focused on breath.	I smelled flowers on table.	6
Wednesday	I'm not doing this right. I'm a loser.	Frustrated, tense.	Focused on feeling of cool air coming into nostrils.	Focused on sound of fan in the next room.	8

Ways to Anchor Here, Not There

Now that you've introduced yourself to the act of observing in a present-focused, nonjudgmental way, you might have noticed something: It's not easy staying in the present moment. Your mind tends to swing away from the present moment, and it can be difficult to swing it back. An anchor to the present moment can help.

Anything can serve as an anchor to the present: your breath, an activity, or even a word. However, take care how you use your anchor to the present. Don't use your anchor to run away or distract yourself from your anxious or depressed feelings. That's just more of the problem. Instead, the purpose of an anchor is to bring your attention and awareness to the present moment when you're feeling anxious or down. Once you shift your attention to the anchor, check in with the parts of your emotional response: mind, body, and actions. Once you're aware of your emotional response in this way, you can more easily determine whether it's an accurate reflection of what is going on at that specific moment in time.

If you meditate, you know the value of the breath as an anchor to the present moment. There may be no better anchor than the breath. No matter where you go, there you are and there it is. Breathing mindfully invites feelings of peace and acceptance. As you accept your feelings, you no longer fight them, and as counterintuitive as this feels, it works. Accepting whatever is happening in the moment—including whatever you're feeling—is a powerful way to quiet your emotions.

When you breathe mindfully, you attend to your breath without judgment. To attend to your breath in this way, anchor your attention on some part of your body that the breath touches. You might observe the feel of the air coming through your nose or mouth, or the rise and fall of your abdomen, or the way your ribs expand and contract with each breath in and out.

Once you've anchored your attention to the present moment in this way, let go of each thought, each feeling, and each sensation that enters your awareness. Do this by acknowledging the thought, feeling, or sensation as it arises (perhaps saying gently to yourself, "thought," "feeling," "sensation") and then returning your attention to your breath.

As you practice mindfully breathing, you'll notice your attention wander away from your breath to greet thoughts—maybe even getting lost in them for a little while. Don't feel discouraged or frustrated by this. This is normal and natural. Our minds naturally distract us from what we're doing. Even people who have meditated for many years find that their minds wander. Perhaps through practice, you'll learn to rest your attention a bit more on your breath rather than on your thoughts. But you'll never be able to get rid of a thought you don't want or fix your attention on your breath and keep it there. In fact, that's not the goal of mindfulness.

The goal of mindfulness is to change the way you relate to your thoughts. Instead of struggling with your thoughts, you learn to catch yourself when you're caught up in them, let go of them, and return to the present moment. In a sense, you learn to let go of pieces of your emotional responses when they arise—as they inevitably will—and return to the present moment.

Exercise: Breath as an Anchor

Practice breathing mindfully three times a day. Start with just two minutes of practice each time, and add a minute as you become more comfortable and confident, up to five minutes. Once you reach five minutes per practice, try bundling these five-minute practices into a single fifteen-minute practice. The benefits of these longer periods of mindful breathing can last for many hours, which make it well worth the time you set aside to do it. To help you remember to practice, link it to something you do every day—for example, before you shower, before you eat, or after you brush your teeth.

Here's a simple script to help you learn to anchor to the present moment through breathing mindfully. After you complete the exercise, answer the questions that follow.

> *Close your eyes or fix your eyes on a spot in front of you, and bring your attention to your breathing. Observe your breathing as if you've never encountered breathing before. Observe your breathing as if you're a curious scientist who wishes to observe the process closely without judgment.*
>
> *Notice the air as it comes in your nostrils and down to the bottom of your lungs, and notice the air as it comes back out again. Notice how the air is slightly cooler as it goes in and slightly warmer as it goes out.* [Pause for 5 seconds.] *Notice the gentle rise and fall of your shoulders with each breath* [pause for 5 seconds] *and the slow rise and fall of your rib cage* [pause for 5 seconds] *and the comfortable rise and fall of your abdomen.* [Pause for 5 seconds.]
>
> *Rest your attention on one of these areas now, whichever you prefer: on the breath moving in and out of your nostrils, on the gentle rise and fall of your shoulders, or the easy rise and fall of your abdomen. Rest your attention on this spot and notice the in and out of the breath.* [Pause for 10 seconds.]
>
> *Whatever feelings, urges, or sensations arise, whether pleasant or unpleasant, gently acknowledge them and let them be—gently acknowledge them, as if nodding your head at someone passing by on the street—and return your attention to the breath.* [Pause for 10 seconds.] *Whatever thoughts, images, or memories arise, whether comfortable or uncomfortable, gently acknowledge them and let them be. Let them come and go as they please. Then return your attention to the breath.* [Pause for 10 seconds.]
>
> *From time to time, your attention will wander away from the breath, and each time this happens, notice what distracted you, and then bring your attention back to the breath. No matter how often you drift off into your thoughts, whether a hundred times or a thousand, simply note what distracted you and return your attention to the breath.* [Pause for 10 seconds.]
>
> *Again and again, your mind will wander away from the breath. This is normal and natural, and happens to everyone. Our minds naturally distract us from what we're doing, so each time this happens, gently acknowledge it, notice what distracted you, and then return your attention to the breath.* [Pause for 10 seconds.] *If frustration, boredom, anxiety, or other feelings arise, simply acknowledge them, and return your attention to the breath.* [Pause for 10 seconds.] *No matter how often your mind wanders, gently acknowledge it, note what distracted you, and return your attention to the breath.*

Write down the thoughts or images that repeatedly came into your mind. Which thoughts or images were the most difficult to direct your attention away from?

____

____

Write down the physical sensations that drew your attention away from your breath. Which physical sensations were the most difficult to direct your attention away from?

____

____

Now, that you've practiced mindfulness in several ways, it's time to apply mindfulness to your anxious or depressed feelings. Again, mindfulness helps you observe these emotions in the present moment so that the feelings don't sweep you up and carry you away.

Exercise: Mindfulness of Your Emotions

To learn to observe your emotions mindfully, observe the feeling as if the feeling is completely new to you. Observe the shadings of the feeling—the ups and downs along with the qualities of the entire experience. Become deeply curious about this emotional experience that you've worked desperately to avoid. Try to describe the feeling as fully as possible, as if you were a scientist trying to record this normal and natural emotion. Don't try to suppress or distract yourself from the feeling. Let it be whatever it is and as strong as it is. And don't judge the feeling or yourself for having it.

As you observe your feelings, you'll notice *action urges*—an impetus to do something. These urges are a natural part of your anxious and depressed feelings. The urge to withdraw when you're feeling depressed. The urge to leave a situation when you're feeling anxious. Just watch these urges without acting on them.

Here's how to apply mindfulness to your feelings:

1. **Acknowledge and label the feeling.** Observe it briefly to see how strong it is and whether other emotions (such as anxiety, anger, guilt, shame, sadness) are mixed in.

2. **Observe your breath.** Bring your attention to your abdomen while you breathe in and out.

3. **Label your thoughts.** When thoughts arise, label them and return your attention to your breath as you observe other parts of the feeling.

4. **Open your awareness.** Like the lens of a camera, open your awareness to become more conscious of the space around you. Watch for other emotions, for sensations in your body, as well as the

sights, sounds, and smells outside your body. Then move your awareness beyond the room you're in to the building, to the neighborhood, to the town in which you live.

5. **Notice your place in space.** As you open your awareness, observe the feeling in the context of your body within the larger world around you.

6. **Continue to observe.** Continue to watch the feeling until the feeling subsides, as waves do, or until the feeling changes into another feeling, or until you've practiced enough.

On the lines below, list the thoughts, physical sensations, and action urges you noticed while you practiced this exercise:

____

____

____

____

____

The point of observing a feeling is to learn to let the feeling be what it is. If you have felt anxious or depressed for many years, you likely have developed a push-away attitude to these emotions. This push-away attitude is a sign of inflexible attention. Learning to observe emotions helps you to develop a new attitude toward your anxious or depressed feelings. Rather than running away from a feeling, you learn to turn toward it and watch the emotion rise and fall, like a wave. Through mindfulness, you learn the power of turning toward your anxious and depressed feelings in the present moment with openness and acceptance. Over the next few days, practice applying mindfulness to moments when you're feeling anxious or depressed.

Bring Mindfulness into Your Daily Life

In addition to setting aside a specific time to practice mindfulness every day, you can practice mindfulness informally by applying an observing, curious, nonjudgmental attitude toward typical things you do every day. Doing the dishes, taking a shower, climbing the stairs, walking to the bus stop, eating lunch, or hugging someone you love are examples of the small things you might do every day but perhaps not in a mindful way. These activities make terrific anchors to the present moment. Let's try working with them now.

Exercise: Anchor to Daily Activities

Often the best activities for present-focused anchors are physical—not mental—so that you can observe every detail of the experience. It doesn't matter what activity you choose, so long as it's brief, you can do it every day, and you can use all your senses as you do it (smell, taste, touch, hearing, sight). For example, as you walk from the front door to the kitchen, focus on the smells of your house. Observe the pattern in the carpet or drapes. Feel the weight beneath your feet and the sound you make walking across the carpet or floor. Pay attention to where you place your keys or lunch bag and the sounds they make as you drop them there.

As you practice mindfulness during these activities, observe any thoughts that enter your mind. Notice them and label them, then return your attention to the sensory details of the activity. As your attention drifts away, gently nudge it back to the sensory details of what you're doing at that moment. You might want to use signs or signals to remind you to act mindfully. For example, if you plan to eat breakfast mindfully, make a paper placemat on which you've written "Mindful." If you plan to walk up the stairs mindfully, place a sign on the step to remind you. If you wish to practice walking mindfully home, pick a house or storefront along the way that's your "mindful" spot to remind you to shift your attention to mindful walking.

During the next few days, try anchoring to activities. You might want to begin with just a single daily activity and practice it for a week. Later, add another activity and another. Try to plan activities throughout the day—morning, afternoon, evening—so that you're practicing mindful activities all day long.

On the lines below, list the mindful activities you practiced. Which activities were the easiest and most difficult to anchor to? Why?

____

____

____

____

Next, we'll explore two more informal mindfulness practices that can increase your attentional flexibility.

Exercise: Anchor to "And"

Another way to anchor to the present moment is to anchor to a word or phrase. For example, on your drive to work you can listen for the word "and" as you listen to the lyrics of a song or to a newscast. As you stand in a crowded restaurant or ride the bus to work, listen for "and" in the conversations around you. As you walk to work, notice "and" on the signs and billboards around you. This simple skill pulls you back to the present moment.

Over the next few days, try anchoring to "and." Then describe several ways you anchored to "and." Which activities were the easiest and most difficult to anchor to? Why?

Exercise: Anchor to One Thing at a Time

Another way to practice mindfulness is to anchor to something you're doing. Just be sure you're only doing one thing. If you're like most people, you seldom do one thing at a time. You scroll your newsfeed while eating breakfast. You wash dishes while listening to the radio. You brush your teeth while thinking about yesterday or tomorrow.

Throughout every day there are many opportunities to build flexible attention by slowing down and doing just one thing at a time—and doing this in a mindful way. When you're feeling overwhelmed and anxious, or exhausted and down, slow down and pay attention to the activity you're doing. Notice only that activity and nothing else. Get curious about the activity in order to go deeply into it. What is the experience of washing dishes truly like? Notice the feeling of the water on your hands. Notice the bubbles pop on the surface of the water. Notice the sound of running water. Notice the particular motions in your hand, arm, and back that go into washing a dish.

Anchoring your attention to a single thing helps shift your attention from the thoughts about the future or the past that are upsetting you. Anchoring to the details of one thing slows down your mind.

During the next few days, try anchoring your attention to one activity. Then, describe several activities you practiced doing mindfully. Which activities were the easiest and most difficult to anchor to? Why?

Long Story Short

Mindfulness is an important skill that works against the inflexible attention that maintains your anxious and depressed feelings. Learning to unhook from your emotional responses will quiet your mind, calm your body, and help you see the world and yourself more clearly and accurately. As you learn to anchor to the present moment, remember:

- Building flexible attention counters the habitual what-ifs about the future that make you anxious. It also counters the habitual regrets and disappointments about the past that bring you down.
- Building flexible attention increases your confidence that you can tolerate your strong anxious and depressed feelings.
- Building flexible attention enhances your awareness that emotions come and go—that what *feels* true in the moment can change to what *is* true about the past, the future, and you.

Chapter 6

Build Flexible Thinking

Inflexible thinking contributes to excessive anxiety and depression. As you learned in chapter 2, inflexible thinking makes it difficult for you to step outside your emotional responses to see things as they really are. It's the inflexibility of your thoughts—rather than the thoughts themselves—that fuel your anxious and depressed feelings. With a little practice, you can learn to open your mind to see your life and yourself in a more balanced and helpful way. Opening your mind is an important step in opening your life.

Automatic Thoughts

Our minds interpret and assign meaning to events automatically in order to improve our ability to live in a complicated and fast-paced world. For example, as you walk down the sidewalk and hear the sound of a skateboarder quickly approaching, it's very important that your mind focus on the speed and direction of the skateboard rather than the color of the skateboard or whether the rider is tall or short. Focusing on the speed and direction of the skateboard will help you quickly decide whether this situation is dangerous or not, so that you can step out of the way or continue walking.

Biases, Interpretations, Meanings

In any given situation or event, your mind automatically focuses on one aspect over another—and in this way, it forms certain automatic information-processing *biases*. For example, at the birthday party Janine attends with her children, one of the other mothers smiles at Janine and says, "That's a beautiful sweater. I love the color on you. Did you know that you have a little cheese dip on the sleeve?" The mother then leaves to get a damp towel for Janine to clean it. As the mother walks away, all Janine can focus on is the woman pointing to the cheese dip on her sweater. Because Janine is depressed, her mind focuses on one thing (usually negative) over another (usually positive). In this case, she focuses on the remark about the cheese dip over the compliment on her sweater.

In addition to focusing on one thing instead of another, your mind automatically *interprets* events. For example, Janine might interpret the mother pointing to the cheese dip on her sweater as proof that she's incompetent ("What's wrong with me? I can't even eat without making a mess").

Alternatively, Janine might interpret the comment to mean that the woman likes her and wants to be her friend ("She really likes the color of my sweater. She appreciates my artistic side. And I'm glad she pointed out that cheese dip and tried to help me clean it off"). Or she could choose not to interpret the comment in any significant way at all and just let it go ("Wow, that was kind of embarrassing. But this sort of thing happens to everyone. It's no big deal").

Last, your mind assigns *meaning* to events that make them seem more important than they really are. For example, Janine takes the comment about the cheese dip on her sweater to mean that she's messy and a horrible mother ("I'm a lazy slob and can't take care of myself or my kids"). Alternatively, Janine can see the cheese dip as a single event ("Yikes! Kid birthday parties are crazy, and it's difficult to pay attention. Next time, I'll be more careful when eating at the snack table") rather than a character flaw.

If you struggle with excessive anxious or depressed feelings, you have developed an automatic and inflexible tendency to interpret events in fearful or pessimistic ways. This inflexible pattern of thinking makes it difficult for you to step outside your anxious or depressed feelings to see the world and yourself in more reasonable and helpful ways.

Hot Thoughts

Your pattern of inflexible thinking likely includes many different automatic thoughts, but not all thoughts are the same. Some thoughts or appraisals cause you to feel more anxious or down than others, in part because some appraisals have more negative meanings than others do. *Hot thoughts* are the appraisals that intensify your anxious and depressed feelings. It's essential that you first learn to identify the hot thought. Once you identify the hot thought, you'll be able to effectively examine whether that thought makes sense in a given situation.

The *downward arrow technique* is a simple strategy that you can use to identify a hot thought (Burns 1980). It consists of taking a particular depressed or anxious thought and exploring what fuels that thought until you identify the most fundamental thing you believe or fear. This is a bit like peeling an onion, whereby one thought or appraisal is just beneath the one above it.

Using the Identify My Hot Thought Worksheet, Rosario identified in just a few steps her hot thought. She started by writing down her automatic thought or appraisal: "What if he sees that I'm blushing?" Then she answered the question most directly linked to the automatic thought: "What would happen if this were true?" Rosario wrote down the answer: "He'll think that I'm weird." She then answered the question most directly linked to that thought: "What would happen next?" She answered: "If he thinks I'm weird, then he'll tell all the other teachers and staff." Rosario continues asking and answering until she arrives at the final underlying thought, which seems like an extreme reaction to her fear of blushing while giving a presentation. That's what makes it a hot thought!

Rosario's Identify My Hot Thought Worksheet

Automatic thought: What if he sees me blushing?

- If this were true, what would this mean about me (or other people)?
- What would happen if this were true?
- What would happen next?
- Why does this matter to me?

Underlying thought: He'll think I'm weird.

- If this were true, what would this mean about me (or other people)?
- What would happen if this were true?
- What would happen next?
- Why does this matter to me?

Underlying thought: If he thinks I'm weird, he'll tell other teachers.

- If this were true, what would this mean about me (or other people)?
- What would happen if this were true?
- What would happen next?
- Why does this matter to me?

Underlying thought: I'll have to quit my job.

- If this were true, what would this mean about me (or other people)?
- What would happen if this were true?
- What would happen next?
- Why does this matter to me?

Underlying thought: I'll never find a job I love. I'll live the rest of my life miserable and depressed.

Now, take a couple of your ABCs of Emotion Worksheets (see chapter 3) and use the blank Identify My Hot Thought Worksheet to identify some of your hot thoughts. As you'll see, your initial automatic thought usually tells only part of the story. As you peel back the layers of your initial automatic thought, you'll begin to understand why you feel so anxious or depressed.

Identify My Hot Thought Worksheet

Automatic thought: ______________________________

- If this were true, what would this mean about me (or other people)?
- What would happen if this were true?
- What would happen next?
- Why does this matter to me?

Underlying thought: ______________________________

- If this were true, what would this mean about me (or other people)?
- What would happen if this were true?
- What would happen next?
- Why does this matter to me?

Underlying thought: ______________________________

- If this were true, what would this mean about me (or other people)?
- What would happen if this were true?
- What would happen next?
- Why does this matter to me?

Underlying thought: ______________________________

- If this were true, what would this mean about me (or other people)?
- What would happen if this were true?
- What would happen next?
- Why does this matter to me?

Underlying thought: ______________________________

Thinking Traps

A *thinking trap* is your tendency to repeatedly and automatically interpret events in particular ways. Thinking traps are like ruts in the road worn deep through years of interpreting things in the same way over and over. It's not always easy to steer out of a rut, even when you want to. Therefore, thinking traps are the hallmark of inflexible thinking—and as you know by now, inflexible thinking contributes to the intensity and persistence of your anxious and depressed feelings.

To see how thinking traps work, recall Janine and the cheese dip incident. Who hasn't dropped a bit of food on their laps or run their sleeve through dip? It helps when someone points out the mistake so that we can be a bit more careful at the buffet table. However, this incident triggered Janine's depressive feelings because she overfocused on the mistake and ignored the mother's compliment.

In this way, Janine filtered out important information that would have helped her feel better (or at least not as depressed) if she'd taken it in. Once Janine felt down, other unhelpful thoughts ran through her mind: "What's wrong with me? I can't even eat without making a mess." She became swept up in an inflexible pattern of thinking that intensified and maintained her depression.

Perhaps the most important step in building flexible thinking is to know when you've slipped into the old, inflexible thinking traps that fuel your anxious or depressed feelings. There are many types of thinking traps, but the most common traps that fuel intense anxious and depressed feelings are: *jumping to conclusions*, *doom and gloom*, and *thinking the worst*.

Jumping to Conclusions

When you jump to conclusions, you overestimate the likelihood that something bad will happen: that your marriage will fail, that you'll catch a horrible disease, that you'll die from a panic attack, or that nothing good will ever happen to you. When the bad event *is likely to happen*, this is a very helpful pattern of thinking because it prepares you to deal with the bad event or perhaps to avoid it altogether. This is your emotional mind at its best.

However, at its worst, your mind repeatedly predicts bad things that *don't* occur. You therefore feel overly anxious and depressed for no reason. For example, Rosario persistently jumps to the conclusion that people can see when she's blushing without any evidence that her blushing is noticeable to other people. Similarly, Janine jumps to the conclusion that she'll always be alone because her marriage failed, without considering the good reasons that indicate she'll one day find a new meaningful relationship.

Write several examples of jumping-to-conclusion thoughts that run through your mind when you're feeling anxious or depressed.

____

____

____

____

____

Doom and Gloom

If the pattern of jumping to conclusions isn't enough to make you needlessly anxious or depressed, you might then overfocus on the false conclusions and thereby exclude evidence that challenges these conclusions. For example, when Rosario jumps to the conclusion that people will notice that she's blushing, she overfocuses on that particular conclusion rather than considering other explanations or interpretations (for example, people don't appear to notice that she's blushing at all). This pattern of predicting *doom* at every turn is the way Rosario tends to interpret or view things. And when she's focused on doom at every turn, it's difficult for Rosario to see evidence that counters the conclusion that makes her anxious. People speak to her. They smile at her. Most important, they almost never ask if she's feeling okay, which would be a natural question if someone saw that Rosario's face looks flush.

Then there's Janine, who is swept up in a pattern of thinking that creates hopelessness and *gloom*. When she thinks of her ex-husband, she focuses on the qualities she likes about him and filters out the many negative qualities that made their life together difficult. When she thinks about herself as a mother, she sees only those times when she was irritable and too tired to play with her children, and excludes the many more times she read to them, played cards with them, and took them to the zoo. The more time Rosario and Janine spend focusing on certain conclusions and not others, the longer they'll feel overly anxious and depressed.

Write several examples of doom-and-gloom thoughts that run through your mind when you're feeling anxious or depressed.

____

____

____

____

____

Thinking the Worst

This thinking trap is your tendency to think that the worst possible thing will happen. Thinking the worst means that your mind tends to catastrophize. In other words, when the bad thing happens—and you believe it surely will—it will be absolutely horrible. For example, Rosario believes that if she blushes—and she believes that she surely will—her principal will fire her because blushing is a sign that she's incompetent. Rosario believes that the worst is very likely to happen even though a much less disastrous outcome is more likely. For Janine, the worst conclusion that runs through her mind is that she'll live the rest of her life alone and lonely.

Furthermore, when you think the worst possible thing is absolutely going to happen, you also believe that you won't be able handle it. For example, if you fail a test, you might believe that you'll never recover from this setback—that you'll curl up in a ball and give up on school and your dreams, that you won't be able to handle your disappointment or the opinions of your teachers, parents, or friends. But we all experience setbacks. We all make mistakes, and bad things do happen. Most of the time, we're able to cope with these events. However, when you underestimate your ability to cope, then even a little thing can become a catastrophe—at least in your emotional mind.

Nia's belief that she couldn't cope with losing Pete, her boyfriend, makes it difficult for her to enjoy time with him. Although Nia and Pete get along well, relationships do end, and for Nia to believe that she couldn't cope with the loss only makes something that would be difficult into something that's truly catastrophic. Janine's belief that she can't handle living without a partner makes her life feel unbearable and hopeless.

Write several examples of thinking-the-worst thoughts that run through your mind when you're feeling anxious or depressed.

____

____

____

____

____

Again, it's not that these patterns of thinking are bad or terrible. It's only that these thinking patterns are *inflexible*—and therefore, once you fall into the thinking pattern, it's difficult for you to shift out of it. You're then stuck in the cycle of anxious and depressed feelings that hold you back and make your life overwhelming and difficult. The first step in building more flexible thinking is to learn to notice when you've fallen into one of these thinking traps and label which one it is.

To get an idea of how to do this, look at Janine's Identify My Thinking Traps Worksheet on the following page. Notice that she felt anxious, depressed, and even guilty, depending what she thought in the situations.

And after you look at the example, it's your turn. Write down your automatic thoughts (what is going through your mind) each time you feel anxious or depressed, and describe the situation you were in when this happened. Then, place a checkmark next to the thinking trap that best describes the automatic thought. At times, one or more thinking traps might contribute to your emotional response. If that's the case, check all that apply.

Janine's Identify My Thinking Traps Worksheet

Date/Time	Situation	Hot Automatic Thought	Feeling	Thinking Trap
April 2, 6 p.m.	At parent's place, see the way Jackson looks at my sister Susan.	I'll never find someone who loves me like Jackson loves Susan.	Sad.	☐ Jumping to conclusions ☑ Doom and gloom ☐ Thinking the worst
April 4, 1:30 p.m.	I'm buying groceries, Laura invites me to a party on Friday.	I can't stand people knowing that Ben left me. They'll think I'm a loser.	Anxious.	☑ Jumping to conclusions ☐ Doom and gloom ☐ Thinking the worst
April 4, 5 p.m.	Playing checkers with Jake. He's laughing and having a great time.	I'm a horrible mom. My kids need me, and all I can think about is myself.	Guilty.	☐ Jumping to conclusions ☐ Doom and gloom ☑ Thinking the worst

Identify My Thinking Traps Worksheet

Date/Time	Situation	Hot Automatic Thought	Feeling	Thinking Trap
				☐ Jumping to conclusions ☐ Doom and gloom ☐ Thinking the worst
				☐ Jumping to conclusions ☐ Doom and gloom ☐ Thinking the worst
				☐ Jumping to conclusions ☐ Doom and gloom ☐ Thinking the worst

Don't Blame Your Mind

Once you become aware of your thinking traps, you might blame your mind for working this way. You might think, "I can't believe I fell into that thinking trap again. I'm such an idiot." This only makes things worse. The more you blame yourself for the way your mind works, the more you'll try to control or reject these thoughts, and the more rigid your thinking pattern becomes.

Rather than blaming your mind by saying things like, "I just keep thinking the same thing over and over. I'm such a loser," try accepting your mind and its amazing ability to generate thoughts in this way. Remind yourself that what you're thinking is one way of thinking and that there are other ways to think too. The mindfulness strategies you learned in chapter 5 will help you to do that. As you meditate, thank your mind for these thoughts rather than blaming your mind for doing what minds do.

Write what goes through your head when you're blaming your mind for falling into a thinking trap.

____

____

____

Now, reframe what you just wrote. Write a sentence or two that accepts that your mind works this way and that you are not at fault (for example, "It's not my fault that my mind sometimes works this way. I'm doing my best to think differently about things and that will take a little time").

____

____

____

Exercise: Take the Long Way Around a Thought

In addition to mindfully observing an unhelpful automatic thought, you can also distance yourself from it by "taking the long way around" it. The long way around a thought is when you describe the thought, physical sensation, or urge with a longer, wordier description—which lessens the impact the thought has on you.

For example, you can distance yourself from the short, scary anxious thought, "What if I lose my job?" by taking the long way around it: "My mind once again is having that very familiar and oh-so-scary thought—a thought that enters my mind over and over again without variation and without merit—that I might lose my job." Similarly, you can take the long way around a thought that tends to bring you down: "My mind once again is having that very familiar and oh-so-depressing thought—a thought that enters my mind over and over again in the same way without truth or importance—that I will never be happy again."

Taking the long way around a thought creates some distance between you and the thought so that you can view the thought and the situation with unclouded eyes. Now you try it. Write a typical thought that comes into your mind when you're feeling anxious or depressed.

____

____

Now, write four to six sentences that take the long way around the thought.

____

____

____

____

____

____

Flexible Thinking Strategies

There are particular thinking strategies you can use to counteract the three most common thinking traps people with excessive anxiety and depression fall into: jumping to conclusions, doom and gloom, and thinking the worst. These three traps are united by a common factor: they reflect an inflexible approach to interpreting events. Each of the flexible thinking strategies you'll learn will help you develop a more pliable approach to interpreting events—and thereby decrease the intensity and duration of your anxious or depressed reactions to those events.

Exercise: Catch It, Check It, Change It

This flexible thinking strategy is easy to learn and combines two skills (identifying a hot automatic thought and challenging a hot automatic thought) that you've already learned. Use the Catch It, Check It, Change It Worksheet that follows to practice this flexible thinking skill.

Step 1: Catch it. This means that you catch the hot automatic thought that's fueling your anxious or depressed feelings. So when you feel anxious or depressed, check your thoughts. What are you thinking? Are those the thoughts that are making you feel depressed or anxious? Which of the thoughts is the hot automatic thought? If you're not certain whether a thought is hot or not, use the downward arrow technique. Write this hot automatic thought in the space provided on the worksheet.

If you caught several hot automatic thoughts, write down all of them.

Step 2: Identify the emotion. Then rate the intensity of the emotion from 0 to 100, whereby 100 is the most intensely anxious or depressed you can imagine feeling, and 0 is not feeling anxious or depressed at all.

Step 3: Rate the strength of the belief. Assess how strongly you believe that the hot automatic thought is true from 0 to 100 percent, whereby 100 percent means you completely believe the automatic thought is true, and 0 percent means that you don't at all believe the automatic thought is true. If you have more than one thought, rate them all. The hottest of the hot automatic thoughts will be the one you believe the most strongly is true. You'll focus on that automatic thought because the stronger you believe the truth of an automatic thought, the more intense the feeling associated with the thought.

Step 4: Check it. Notice if the hot automatic thought is a thinking trap. Is the thought an example of jumping to conclusions, predicting either doom or gloom, or thinking the worst? There's considerable overlap among the three thinking traps, so it's okay to checkmark all of them if they all seem to fit.

Step 5: Change it. Now you'll change the hot thought by realistically examining the likelihood that the event or outcome will happen or is true. Is the thought really true? Do you have evidence that tells you it's true? How about evidence that the thought is false? Would a friend think about this event or situation in the same way? Does this thought make your life easier or more difficult? Is this thought helping or hindering your life goals?

Questioning your thinking can be difficult because these thoughts are likely familiar and "feel" true. However, just because something *feels* true doesn't mean it *is* true. Write these new, more helpful thoughts in the space provided on the worksheet.

Step 6: Re-rate the emotion. Now that you've had a chance to reflect on the accuracy or helpfulness of the thought, re-rate the emotion from 0 to 100, whereby 100 is the most intensely anxious or depressed you can imagine feeling, and 0 is not feeling anxious or depressed at all.

Step 7: Re-rate the strength of the belief. Assess whether you believe that the automatic thought is true from 0 to 100 percent, whereby 100 percent means you completely believe that the automatic thought is true, and 0 percent means that you don't at all believe the automatic thought is true.

That's it!

To help you get started, look at the worksheets Mateo and Janine completed. Mateo, who is anxious, identified all three thinking traps (doom, jumping to conclusions, thinking the worst). He then quickly countered the anxious automatic thoughts with new thoughts or coping responses that not only were more accurate but were more helpful too. In the process, Mateo added some flexibility into his thinking and felt less anxious.

Janine, who is depressed, identified a hot automatic thought that primarily focused on the negative. This is her gloom thinking trap. Janine was able to think about her thinking. In the process, she stepped out of her pattern of overfocusing on her contribution to the breakup of her marriage. She felt much better because her thinking was now both balanced and accurate.

Mateo's Catch It, Check It, Change It Worksheet

Instructions: You can learn to catch, check, and change your thoughts that make you feel anxious, angry, sad, or guilty. In the "Catch it" row, write the thought that is troubling you. Then, in the "Check it" row, write the thinking trap for the thought you caught. Now, go through the questions in the "Change it" section and see if you can reason your way through the thought and feel better.

Triggering Situation	Attending networking event with partners.		
Catch it	What words, phrases, or images went through my mind just before or while I was feeling anxious or depressed? What is my worst fear? What do these thoughts mean about me, my life, or my future?	I'm going to faint in front of partners and that will end my career.	
Emotions	Terrified, anxious.	**Intensity of emotion (0–100)**	80
		Strength of belief (0–100%)	90%
Check it	**Identify the thinking traps.**	☑ Jumping to conclusions ☑ Doom and gloom ☑ Thinking the worst	
Change it	Am I 100 percent certain this event or consequence will happen? Could there be any other explanations? What's the evidence that this belief is true? Is the situation really so important? What would I tell a friend who was in this situation? Is there a more helpful way to think about this? Is there another view that better fits the evidence?	I've felt dizzy hundreds of times and I've never passed out. Even if I did pass out, the partners wouldn't fire me. They'd probably ask if I was okay, and I'd tell them I'm tired because of the new baby. The dizziness is my anxiety. It doesn't mean I'm going to faint.	
Emotions	Anxious.	**Intensity of emotion (0–100)**	20
		Strength of belief (0–100%)	35%

Janine's Catch It, Check It, Change It Worksheet

Instructions: You can learn to catch, check, and change your thoughts that make you feel anxious, angry, sad, or guilty. In the "Catch it" row, write the thought that is troubling you. Then, in the "Check it" row, write the thinking trap for the thought you caught. Now, go through the questions in the "Change it" section and see if you can reason your way through the thought and feel better.

Triggering Situation	Remembering Jack moving his things out of the house.		
Catch it	What words, phrases, or images went through my mind just before or while I was feeling anxious or depressed? What is my worst fear? What do these thoughts mean about me, my life, or my future?	It's all my fault that Jack wasn't happy. I'm such a loser. He was right to leave me.	
Emotions	Sad, hopeless.	**Intensity of emotion (0–100)**	90
		Strength of belief (0–100%)	80%
Check it	**Identify the thinking traps.**	☐ Jumping to conclusions ☑ Doom and gloom ☑ Thinking the worst	
Change it	Am I 100 percent certain this event or consequence will happen? Could there be any other explanations? What's the evidence that this belief is true? Is the situation really so important? What would I tell a friend who was in this situation? Is there a more helpful way to think about this? Is there another view that better fits the evidence?	Jack said that he's having a midlife crisis and it's not about me. I wasn't happy either and had thoughts of leaving, so maybe it's not completely my fault. I'd tell a friend that it's almost never just one person's fault when people break up. Jack was unhappy in his career and says he's not cut out to be a father.	
Emotions	Sad, guilty.	**Intensity of emotion (0–100)**	35
		Strength of belief (0–100%)	30%

Catch It, Check It, Change It Worksheet

Instructions: You can learn to catch, check, and change your thoughts that make you feel anxious, angry, sad, or guilty. In the "Catch it" row, write the thought that is troubling you. Then, in the "Check it" row, write the thinking trap for the thought you caught. Now, go through the questions in the "Change it" section and see if you can reason your way through the thought and feel better.

Triggering Situation			
Catch it	What words, phrases, or images went through my mind just before or while I was feeling anxious or depressed? What is my worst fear? What do these thoughts mean about me, my life, or my future?		
Emotions		**Intensity of emotion (0–100)**	
		Strength of belief (0–100%)	
Check it	**Identify the thinking traps.**	☐ Jumping to conclusions ☐ Doom and gloom ☐ Thinking the worst	
Change it	Am I 100 percent certain this event or consequence will happen? Could there be any other explanations? What's the evidence that this belief is true? Is the situation really so important? What would I tell a friend who was in this situation? Is there a more helpful way to think about this? Is there another view that better fits the evidence?		
Emotions		**Intensity of emotion (0–100)**	
		Strength of belief (0–100%)	

Flexible Thinking Strategies for Jumping to Conclusions

When you jump to conclusions you tend to predict events in a certain way. We all do this and, therefore, we all have a predictometer. As you've learned, the problem isn't that you have a predictometer but that it repeatedly predicts inaccurately. In other words, when you struggle with excessive anxiety or depression, you have a predictometer that's inflexible. The next two exercises will help you build some flexibility into your predictometer so that you learn to anticipate events and outcomes more accurately.

Because your pattern of thinking has you trapped in seeing things in a particular way, you might not often stop to ask yourself two important questions: "What is the prediction I'm making?" and "How likely is it that this prediction is accurate?" Sometimes simply realizing the degree your predictometer is out of whack is enough to add some flexibility to your thinking, helping you shift your tendency to overfocus on negative outcomes. Before you begin the next exercise, let's look at how Nia and Janine tracked not only their predictions but also the accuracy of those predictions.

For two weeks, Nia recorded all of her worst-case predictions about finding a job, her health, the welfare of her family, and the state of the world. Of the seven anxious predictions that Nia made, only one came true (her mother caught Nia's cold). Nia continued to use the Predictions Worksheet for several more weeks. As the number of false predictions increased, Nia saw how often she predicted that something bad would happen and how rarely it actually occurred. Learning this helped her take her worries less seriously, which added some flexibility to her thinking.

Nia's Predictions Worksheet

What negative thing will happen and when?	Strength of Your Belief (0–100%)	What really happened?	Check False Predictions (✓)
Doctor will tell me that the mole on my face is cancerous.	85%	The doctor told me that the mole was not cancerous.	✓
Someone will break into my car tonight.	100%	No one broke into my car last night.	✓
Mom will catch my cold and get very sick.	90%	My mother caught my cold and was pretty sick, but she recovered quickly.	
My boss will fire me because I was 10 minutes late.	80%	She asked me to try not to be late again and smiled at me. She didn't fire me.	✓
My boss will fire me because her kids were awake when they returned from dinner.	70%	I explained that I put them to bed and stayed with them but they couldn't fall asleep. My boss was fine and understood. She didn't fire me.	✓
Mom called and I knew she was going to tell me that my sister was in a car accident or something else bad had happened to her.	70%	She chatted with me and told me that my sister and all my family were fine.	✓
I'm so tired I won't be able to do my job.	80%	I was tired but the kids and my boss didn't seem to notice.	✓

If you're depressed, you can overpredict negative outcomes too, such as anticipating you won't enjoy an activity *at all* or that you won't do a task well. Look at Janine's Predictions Worksheet. Janine noticed that she tended to predict that she wouldn't enjoy an activity *at all*, yet the chart shows that she typically enjoyed activities at least a little. Although she certainly didn't enjoy certain things as much as she did before she became depressed, she did enjoy things somewhat. Learning this encouraged Janine to do a little more, and over time she began to feel better.

Janine's Predictions Worksheet

What negative thing will happen and when?	Strength of Your Belief (0–100%)	What really happened?	Check False Predictions (✓)
I won't enjoy scrapbooking with Gloria at all.	95%	There were moments when I really enjoyed scrapbooking and chatting with Gloria.	✓
I won't enjoy playing Go Fish with the kids at all.	90%	The kids were tired, so it was frustrating sometimes, but I did enjoy myself some.	✓
I won't have any fun on girls' night out.	80%	I didn't enjoy myself like the old days, but there were moments when I felt okay.	✓

Exercise: Test the Accuracy of Your Predictions

For the next two weeks, every time you predict a negative outcome, such as losing your job or not enjoying an activity *at all*, record the prediction on the blank Predictions Worksheet. Then, indicate how strongly you believe the prediction (0 to 100 percent, whereby 100 percent means that you believe the prediction is completely accurate), plus what really happened. If your prediction is false, place a checkmark by it.

Predictions Worksheet

What negative thing will happen and when?	Strength of Your Belief (0–100%)	What really happened?	Check False Predictions (✓)

Once you've used your Predictions Worksheet for several weeks, you've likely learned something about your day-to-day tendency to jump to negative conclusions. However, you haven't been thinking this way for just a few weeks or a few months. You've likely been thinking this way for years. Jumping to negative conclusions every day is second nature to you by now. This is what inflexible thinking is all about. To see your true tendency to jump to negative conclusions, it can help to calculate your *validity quotient* (Moses and Barlow 2006): the ratio of valid predictions to total predictions.

Exercise: Calculate Your Validity Quotient

To calculate the validity quotient for your predictions, think back over the last five years (or one or two years) and estimate the total number of times you predicted a particular negative conclusion (for example, "My boss will fire me tomorrow," or "I'll screw up the thing I'm doing"). Enter this number on the My Validity Quotient Worksheet. Next, estimate the total number of times this conclusion came true, and enter this in the worksheet. Now, divide the number of predictions that came true by the total number of negative predictions and multiply by 100, then enter this number on the worksheet. This is your validity quotient. You can calculate your validity quotient for all the negative predictions you made about all kinds of things in the past too.

My Validity Quotient Worksheet

Q1: How many times have I made this prediction in the past five years?	
Q2: How many times in the past five years has this prediction come true?	
Validity quotient (Q2/Q1) x 100%	

Nia calculated the validity quotient for her prediction that her boss would fire her from her job as a nanny. Nia estimated that at least three times a month she predicted that her boss was going to fire her for one thing or another. Three times per month, twelve months per year, for five years—that's 180 scary predictions. Nia had several bosses over the last five years, but none of her bosses had fired her, and she always received very positive recommendations from them. So, her validity quotient was 0/100 or 0 percent.

Nia's 0 percent validity quotient caught her attention. She'd never stopped to consider the accuracy of her predictions. Each prediction seemed very true to her at the time. From then on, Nia used the validity quotient to reset her predictometer when she was feeling anxious. She calculated her validity quotient for other worries (or predictions) too, such as scary predictions about her health, the safety of her family, and her relationship with her boyfriend.

Janine calculated the validity quotient for the prediction that she'd fail at anything she tried. During the past week, the validity quotient was 22 percent; but when she calculated the validity quotient for this prediction for the past year, it was only 5 percent. Janine now saw what little validity this prediction ultimately had, even if it tended to influence how she felt every day. It also occurred to her that the higher percentage during the past week was likely due to her depression, which made it difficult for her to start and complete tasks.

Flexible Thinking Strategies for Doom and Gloom

Doom and gloom means that your emotional mind repeatedly tends to jump to scary or negative interpretations about events and then locks on to them. This is particularly true when the event is ambiguous and therefore could be interpreted in several ways. If you have social anxiety or become very anxious in social situations, you'll understand what happens when you interpret a look on someone's face to mean that they're unhappy with you or that they think you're weird, boring, or annoying. Perhaps they think this or perhaps they don't. How do you know for sure? However, once your emotional mind latches on to a negative interpretation, it's tough to convince your mind to let go of it.

You can learn to loosen your mind's grip on a negative interpretation by teaching it to step back for a second look. You likely can view any situation from other perspectives if you try. For example, in a large theater, there are many views of the stage—such as mezzanine, dress circle, or grand tier—and every view is a bit different. Therefore, each view of the stage creates a different experience. Rosario and Jeanine used the View from the Balcony tool to explore their negative thought habits. Let's look at how they filled out their worksheets before you start yours.

Rosario used the View from the Balcony Worksheet to examine her interpretation that her principal thinks she's weird when he sees that she's blushing. Janine, on the other hand, used the worksheet to examine her interpretation that she ruins everything she tries.

Rosario's View from the Balcony Worksheet

Describe the event or situation.	Speaking to my principal and I feel like I'm blushing.	
Describe my negative view (anxious or depressed interpretation) from the balcony.	He thinks I'm weird because I'm blushing.	**Strength of belief (0–100%)** *Before*
		95%
		Strength of belief (0–100%) *After*
		35%
Other views from the balcony:		**Likelihood this view is true** (0–100%)
He thinks my face is red because I have a fever and am not feeling well.		85%
He thinks my face is red because I'm warm.		85%
He thinks my face is red because I'm tired.		75%
He thinks my face is red because I'm wearing makeup.		65%
He thinks my face is red because I've been moving at a fast pace.		75%

Janine's View from the Balcony Worksheet

<table>
<tr><td>Describe the event or situation.</td><td colspan="2">Made several mistakes when setting up the accounting system to track employee paid time off.</td></tr>
<tr><td rowspan="4">Describe my negative view (anxious or depressed interpretation) from the balcony.</td><td rowspan="4">I ruin everything I try.</td><td>Strength of belief (0–100%)
Before</td></tr>
<tr><td>90%</td></tr>
<tr><td>Strength of belief (0–100%)
After</td></tr>
<tr><td>45%</td></tr>
<tr><td colspan="2">Other views from the balcony.</td><td>Likelihood this view is true
(0–100%)</td></tr>
<tr><td colspan="2">Setting up a new accounting system isn't easy. I'm bound to make some mistakes.</td><td>95%</td></tr>
<tr><td colspan="2">My family asked me to do this because they believe I can do it. They don't expect me not to make mistakes.</td><td>75%</td></tr>
<tr><td colspan="2">I've set up other accounting systems and they work okay.</td><td>85%</td></tr>
<tr><td colspan="2">Although the program had a couple of bugs, overall it worked okay.</td><td>85%</td></tr>
</table>

Exercise: View from the Balcony

Now it's your turn. Imagine that you're in the theater of your mind's interpretations and you're moving from section to section in the theater. From each vantage point, you have a slightly different view of the stage before you. Use the blank View from the Balcony Worksheet and follow these steps to loosen your mind's grip on a particular negative interpretation:

1. Briefly describe the event along with your negative interpretation.
2. Rate the degree to which you believe your interpretation is correct (0 to 100 percent, whereby 100 percent means you completely believe it).
3. Brainstorm five to ten other possible views or explanations for the event.
4. Rate the likelihood that each alternative explanation is true (0 to 100 percent, whereby 100 percent means it's completely true or accurate).
5. Re-rate the degree (0 to 100 percent) that you believe the negative interpretation is correct. Does the strength of your belief decrease as you consider different explanations or views of the event?

View from the Balcony Worksheet

<table>
<tr><td>Describe the event or situation.</td><td colspan="2"></td></tr>
<tr><td rowspan="4">Describe my negative view (anxious or depressed interpretation) from the balcony.</td><td rowspan="4"></td><td>Strength of belief (0–100%)
Before</td></tr>
<tr><td></td></tr>
<tr><td>Strength of belief (0–100%)
After</td></tr>
<tr><td></td></tr>
<tr><td colspan="2">Other views from the balcony.</td><td>Likelihood this view is true
(0–100%)</td></tr>
<tr><td colspan="2"></td><td></td></tr>
<tr><td colspan="2"></td><td></td></tr>
<tr><td colspan="2"></td><td></td></tr>
<tr><td colspan="2"></td><td></td></tr>
</table>

As you practice the View from the Balcony flexible thinking strategy, you'll notice that you're able to consider alternative interpretations faster and easier. This is a sign that you're building more flexible thinking. As your mind becomes more flexible, you'll begin to feel a bit less anxious and depressed, and less often immediately jump to doom and gloom.

Flexible Thinking Strategies for Thinking the Worst

Thinking the worst is your tendency to *overestimate* the likelihood that the worst possible thing will happen and, when it does, that you won't be able to handle it. This second part—*underestimating* the likelihood that you can cope with life events—fuels anxious feelings as well as feelings of despair and hopelessness. In the next two exercises, you'll practice building a plan to cope with the events that we all encounter in the process of living life fully.

Examine How You Coped in the Past

One of the fastest ways to jump back from the worst (de-catastrophize) is to convince yourself that you can handle the worst if it happens. To build confidence that you can cope, it helps to examine how you coped in the past.

Most people have faced difficult times and have coped successfully. Coping successfully, however, doesn't mean that you get through a difficult situation without feeling intensely anxious, sad, frustrated, or hurt. Coping successfully means that you get through a difficult situation as best you can while feeling what you feel.

Some people expect themselves to handle a difficult situation without experiencing uncomfortable feelings. Furthermore, they believe that if they're feeling anxious or sad, for example, they must not be coping well. This couldn't be further from the truth. Coping is about getting through each day until the days get easier. You've likely done this already, and thinking back over the ways you've handled difficult situations can increase your confidence that you'll handle the worst again, if it happens.

Nia completed a Coped in the Past Worksheet for the time she lost her job working for an event planner. She loved the job and was surprised when the company let her go after only ten months. She knew the company was in financial trouble and that was probably the reason she'd been laid off, but she took the layoff very hard and blamed herself.

Nia noticed that an important way she coped with this setback was to lean on her friends and family. She'd been uncomfortable doing this; it was difficult to tell her friends and family that she'd lost her job. However, she could see how helpful it was for her to reach out to others who could offer support and advice on next steps. Realizing that she had a strong and caring support system made the possibility of losing her current job a little less scary.

Nia's Coped in the Past Worksheet

Difficult Situation in the Past

I lost a job I loved.

Ways I Coped with this Situation

I called my mother and sister, who visited me for a few days to help me get my mind off it.

I asked my boss to write a letter of recommendation, and it was a great letter that helped me feel much better.

I called my best friend. She helped me update my résumé and went job hunting with me.

I started free yoga classes at the YWCA, and this helped with my stress.

I called some of my coworkers at the event planning company. They reminded me that I lost my job because the company was downsizing and I was the most recent hire.

Now it's your turn. Use the blank Coped in the Past Worksheet to examine the ways you've handled five situations that were difficult for you. For each crisis, write the specific ways you coped. Write the names of friends you called. Jot down the strategies you used to manage your anxiety or sadness, such as exercise, medications, mindfulness, or hobbies.

Note the personal resources you used to get through the day—your research skills, your ability to negotiate with others, your ability to understand complicated financial matters. Across these crises, which coping strategy helped the most? Did you rely on a particular coping strategy more often than others and was it usually helpful? Did you try any strategy that you've not used before—or used often—and how did that work for you?

Coped in the Past Worksheet

1. Difficult Situation in the Past

____

____

Ways I Coped with this Situation

____

____

____

____

____

____

2. Difficult Situation in the Past

____

____

Ways I Coped with this Situation

____

____

____

____

____

____

3. Difficult Situation in the Past

Ways I Coped with this Situation

4. Difficult Situation in the Past

Ways I Coped with this Situation

5. Difficult Situation in the Past

____

____

Ways I Coped with this Situation

____

____

____

____

____

____

Create a Plan to Jump Back from the Worst

If you have a plan to jump back from the worst, you'll feel less anxious and more hopeful about it, because you'll have a plan to cope with the worst if it happens. Imagine that you're facing the worst—you're facing a serious illness, losing your job, a relationship ending—whatever catastrophe you fear. As difficult as this might be, you're not going to roll over and surrender—even if that's what you believe you would do. You're going to try to cope with it—for yourself and for those who care about you.

Nia filled out the Jump Back from the Worst Plan Worksheet for her chronic worry that her boyfriend, Pete, would break up with her. Pete showed no signs that he was unhappy with Nia or with their relationship, but this didn't stop Nia from running through her mind every day the details of when and how Pete would tell her that he's had enough. In fact, Nia realized that the only thing that rocked her relationship with Pete was that she couldn't stop worrying about a breakup. Nia realized that the real belief that fueled her worry was the belief that she couldn't handle the loneliness and sadness she would feel if she and Pete did break up one day.

Nia's Jump Back from the Worst Plan Worksheet

Describe the worst-case prediction.	My boyfriend leaves me because I'm such a mess.	**Ability to Cope Before (0–100%)** 20%
What are my strengths and resources that will help me cope?	I've had losses before and survived. I'm smart and I can think on my feet. I have a supportive family and network of friends. I meet people easily. People like me and think I'm fun. I work hard. I've a nest egg and I could use that if I had to.	
What can I do to help me cope?	I could use my savings to take a little vacation and hang out with friends. I could use some of the tools I've learned to calm my body and mind. I like the View from the Balcony tool. That will help. I like the mindfulness tools too. They'll help me stay centered and calm. Maybe I'll join a club or do some of the things I never did because Pete wasn't interested. That will help keep my mind off missing him.	
What can I say to myself to help me cope?	I'm a survivor. I've been through breakups before and they're painful but I always got through them. I have friends and family who love me. Pete is a good guy, and even if we break up, I know he'll do it in a decent way. We might even stay friends.	
With whom can I speak or seek support to help me cope?	I'll call my mother and sister and visit them for a week or two. I'll get together with my close friends. They love me.	
Other ways to cope?	Find ways to be around people—coffee shops, parks, other fun things.	**Ability to Cope After (0–100%)** 80%

To create a Jump Back from the Worst Plan, follow these steps:

1. Write a brief description of your worst-case prediction on the worksheet.

2. Rate how confident you feel (0 to 100 percent, whereby 100 means you're completely confident) that you could handle or cope with the worst if it happened.

3. Brainstorm ten or twelve ways you might cope with the worst. For ideas for ways to cope, think back to a hard time in the past. What did you do to get through each day? What tools have you learned in this book to calm your emotional mind and body that might help? What can you say to yourself that would help you cope? Do you have affirmations or inspirational quotes that help you feel better and stronger? What are the things that friends say to you that help, and can you say those things to yourself? Consider your sources of emotional and social support. Which of your family members and friends are good listeners and have helped you through tough times before? Do you have a therapist or physician who's there for you? Perhaps you have a coworker who's good at something that would help you solve a problem that's making life hard for you.

4. Re-rate how confident you feel (0 to 100 percent) that you could handle or cope with the worst if it happened.

Jump Back from the Worst Plan Worksheet

Describe the worst-case prediction.		Ability to Cope Before (0–100%)
What are my strengths and resources that will help me cope?		
What can I do to help me cope?		
What can I say to myself to help me cope?		
With whom can I speak or seek support to help me cope?		
Other ways to cope?		Ability to Cope After (0–100%)

Now that you've created your Jump Back from the Worst Plan, do you feel differently about the worst-case prediction? Do you feel a little less worried about the "catastrophe" if it were to happen? Do you feel less overwhelmed and afraid? Do you feel more hopeful and capable? On the lines below, describe how you feel now when you think about hard times and setbacks:

When the Problem Is What a Thought Means

Our emotional mind gets our attention. It grips us and causes us sometimes to believe that certain thoughts are more important than they really are. This is particularly true when we place a meaning on a thought—when you begin to think that a particular thought means you're in danger or that a particular thought means you're a bad person. It's quite common for people to have odd, strange thoughts that don't make sense. Most people easily let go of these thoughts by telling themselves "That's a silly thought," and soon their minds are on to other things.

However, people with obsessive-compulsive disorder can't easily let go of certain thoughts, particularly when those thoughts enter their mind with great power and force. Thoughts that enter our awareness with power like this are *intrusive*. Some people can have intrusive thoughts that they might hurt a loved one or molest a child. They might have intrusive thoughts that go against their moral or religious beliefs and values, such as unwanted sexual thoughts or images of Satan. These thoughts and images fuel intense feelings of anxiety, guilt, and depression. When people with obsessive-compulsive disorder have intrusive thoughts like these, they try to push the thoughts from their minds, but their (and everyone's) emotional minds don't work that way. The harder we try to push a thought out of our mind, the harder it pushes its way back in.

Write examples of the kinds of nonsensical intrusive thoughts that run through your mind when you're feeling anxious, afraid, guilty, or ashamed:

Thoughts such as these are automatic—in the same way that all thoughts are automatic—but there's an important difference. Intrusive thoughts don't make much sense, and therefore it's not easy or helpful to reason with them. For example, it's not reasonable to reset a predictometer that predicts that you'll die if you touch a counter in your kitchen and don't wash your hands—because the likelihood of that happening is already close to zero. Or if you challenge the thought "I'm a child molester" with the question "What's the worst that can happen and how bad is that?" you're not likely to come back with an answer that reassures you.

Unhook from the Meaning of the Thought

Rather than examining the accuracy or validity of an intrusive thought, it's better to learn to unhook or disengage from it altogether. Let's look at how Malik did this. First he identified his hot intrusive thought. Notice that the hot thought was really what he *believed* it meant to have the intrusive thought "I have germs on my hands." In other words, he believed that having the thought was enough to kill him. That's why intrusive thoughts don't make sense.

Malik's Identify My Hot Intrusive Thought

Automatic thought: I have germs on my hands.

- What do I think having this thought means might happen?
- What do I think having this thought means I might do?
- What do I think having this thought means about me?
- How does having this thought make me feel?

Underlying thought: This thought means I'll get sick.

- What do I think having this thought means might happen?
- What do I think having this thought means I might do?
- What do I think having this thought means about me?
- How does having this thought make me feel?

Underlying thought: This thought means I'll die from some disease.

Now it's your turn. In order to unhook from an intrusive thought, you'll want to unhook from the meaning first. Use the downward arrow technique you learned earlier to identify the hot intrusive thought, but this time ask yourself different questions about the thought—questions focused on what the thought means to you, and not the specifics of the thought's content. "How does having this thought make me feel? What do I think having this thought means about me? What do I think having this thought means might happen?"

Identify My Hot Intrusive Thought

Automatic thought: ______________________________

- What do I think having this thought means might happen?
- What do I think having this thought means I might do?
- What do I think having this thought means about me?
- How does having this thought make me feel?

Underlying thought: ______________________________

- What do I think having this thought means might happen?
- What do I think having this thought means I might do?
- What do I think having this thought means about me?
- How does having this thought make me feel?

Underlying thought: ______________________________

- What do I think having this thought means might happen?
- What do I think having this thought means I might do?
- What do I think having this thought means about me?
- How does having this thought make me feel?

Underlying thought: ______________________________

- What do I think having this thought means might happen?
- What do I think having this thought means I might do?
- What do I think having this thought means about me?
- How does having this thought make me feel?

Underlying thought: ______________________________

Now, look back at Malik's worksheet. Notice how Malik applied the flexible thinking strategies he learned earlier to generate alternative meanings for his intrusive thoughts about germs and disease.

Jumping to Conclusions

What's the likelihood that having the thought "I have germs on my hands" means he'll get sick and die? Malik looked for alternative explanations to what it *meant* to have this thought. He concluded, "I've had thoughts like this before and nothing bad happened. I've even had this thought and couldn't wash my hands and I didn't die. Thoughts don't increase the likelihood that I'll get sick. Thoughts aren't germs."

Write down the jumping-to-conclusion thoughts that run through your mind when you're having a nonsensical intrusive thought:

____

____

____

Are there alternative explanations to what it *means* to have these thoughts? Write those here:

____

____

____

Doom and Gloom

Malik used strategies to shift his overfocus on the *meaning* of the thoughts. He concluded, "Just because I'm having the thought 'I have germs on my hands' many times a day doesn't make the thought important. If I step back and look at this thought—if I look at this thought from the balcony—I realize that this thought isn't any more important than any other thought I have every day. Just because I have this thought many times each day doesn't make the thought truer or increase the likelihood that something bad will happen. When I give the thought 'I have germs on my hands' more importance than it deserves, then the thought grows bigger and scarier in my emotional mind."

Write down the doom-and-gloom thoughts that run through your mind when you're having a nonsensical intrusive thought:

____

____

____

Now, write down some possible alternative explanations to what it might mean to have these thoughts:

____

____

____

Self-Test: Depression, Anxiety, and Stress

You're more than halfway through this workbook, so it's time to check how you're progressing. Please retake the Self-Test that you took in chapter 2. At the end of the workbook, you'll complete the test one last time to see how far you've come.

Long Story Short

The tendency to appraise or interpret events in the same way in spite of evidence to the contrary is the hallmark of inflexible thinking. Remember that your mind is amazing. Your mind has evolved over millions of years to serve you, protect you, and add to the comfort and joy of life. It's only when it slips into a pattern of inflexibility that you suffer. The thinking tools you learned will add flexibility into your thinking so that your mind starts to work for you rather than against you. As you practice these flexible thinking skills, remember:

- Your anxious and depressed predictions are typically wrong, even when they feel right—particularly when they feel right.
- Your future is more hopeful and less dangerous than you think.
- You're more capable and resilient than you believe.

Chapter 7

Build Flexible Action

You've now learned skills to build more flexibility into your attention and thinking. You're likely already noticing that your mind and body are feeling more open and flexible. Perhaps you've even noticed that you feel a bit less anxious or down. Those are signs that you're benefiting from what you've learned and practiced. Now, you come to the last piece of the emotional inflexibility puzzle, and perhaps the most important piece. This last piece—how you act in response to your anxious and depressed feelings—is the focus of this chapter.

Emotion Avoidance

Emotion avoidance is the *act* of avoiding strong negative emotional experiences, such as anxiety and depression. Emotion avoidance actions include two basic types: you directly and fully avoid entering certain situations or participating in certain activities that you've learned trigger your anxious or depressed feelings; and you use subtle strategies to avoid intensifying your anxious or depressed feelings. You use these when you can't avoid or leave a situation, event, or activity that trigger your anxious or depressed feelings.

Exercise: Understand Emotion Avoidance

In this exercise, you'll learn firsthand how difficult it is to avoid emotional experiences. First, think back to an event when you felt intensely anxious or depressed. Choose an event that's difficult for you to think about. Try to remember specific details (who was there, what was happening). In particular, think back to any parts of the event that were particularly upsetting or emotional. What were you doing, thinking, feeling? What physical sensations do you remember? Don't try to avoid any images, thoughts, feelings, or body sensations. Just open yourself to what you remember about this event. Hold this memory in your mind for two minutes.

Now, on the lines provided, describe the emotions you felt and the particular features of the memory that were most difficult for you to think about. Describe any strategies you used to distract from, suppress, or control your experience in order to feel less anxious or depressed:

____

____

____

____

____

____

Now, recall the same memory, but this time use any strategy—including the ones you used in the previous step—to try *not* to think about the event for two minutes. Try as hard as you can to *not* feel the feelings that come up for you. Try as hard as you can to control or suppress any physical sensations associated with your anxious or depressed feelings.

Now, describe what it was like to try not to think about the upsetting event and to avoid feeling anxious or depressed. Describe how well you were able to keep the memory away. Write down which strategy worked the best or worst to avoid your feelings:

____

____

____

____

____

____

This exercise demonstrates how futile it is to avoid internal experiences, such as thoughts, images, and physical sensations. You may have been able to avoid thinking about the event or feeling what you felt during the event, but odds are you could only do this for a brief period. That's because the only way to know whether you're thinking about the event is to check to see whether you're thinking about it. Then, guess what? The moment you check for a particular thought, there it is. The moment you check for a particular physical sensation, there it is. The moment you check whether you're engaging in a mental emotion-avoidance strategy, there it is.

Most often, people avoid "negative" emotions, such as anxiety or depression, but anxious and depressed people avoid "positive" feelings too. For example, if you struggle with excessive anxiety, you might avoid feeling calm or peaceful by running around, keeping busy, and distracting yourself because you believe feeling calm means that you've lowered your guard and then something bad will happen to you.

Similarly, if you're depressed, you might avoid positive feelings because you think you don't deserve to feel happy or joyful. Or you might avoid positive feelings because you believe that although you enjoy yourself in the moment, what's the point, you'll only feel worse later. Therefore, people with chronic and intense anxiety or depression avoid negative and positive feelings using a number of direct and subtle emotion-avoidance strategies. They may avoid activities, objects, or situations that trigger feelings; try to control or dampen feelings; and avoid thoughts or images that intensify anxious and depressed feelings.

Situational Emotion Avoidance

Situational emotion avoidance is the most common type of emotion avoidance. You simply refuse to enter a situation or to engage in an activity that's likely to trigger anxious or depressed feelings. For example, if you're afraid of dogs, you avoid dogs (object) but you also avoid places where you think you're likely to see one, such as the local dog park or pet supply stores (situation).

If you're depressed, you might withdraw to your bedroom and refuse to speak with people or respond to their text messages. Or you might avoid exercising—or any physical activity—because activity triggers fatigue and fatigue triggers thoughts that you're a slob who can't even walk across the room. Similarly, you might avoid starting tasks because you feel overwhelmed and hopeless. Or you might avoid hanging out with friends because being with them triggers thoughts that you're a loser.

Describe the activities, objects, or situations that you avoid because they trigger anxious or depressed feelings:

____

____

____

Subtle Behavioral Emotion Avoidance

If you cannot directly avoid entering a situation or engaging in an activity that you associate with intense anxious or depressed feelings (or if you can't leave the situation for a period of time), you might engage in small and subtle actions to avoid the feelings you're having. In fact, these behaviors might be so subtle that you're not even aware that you're doing them. That's why they're under the category *subtle behavioral emotion avoidance*.

For example, you might stick to "safe" subjects when you speak with people to avoid feeling anxious because you predict you'll say something to upset them. Or you might only try tasks that you're confident that you'll do correctly to avoid triggering depressive thoughts that you're a failure. At times, you might avoid triggering particular physical sensations that are part of your anxious or depressed feelings. For example, if you felt short of breath when you had a panic attack, you might avoid quick movements.

Describe the subtle emotion-avoidance actions you use to dampen or control anxious or depressed feelings:

____

____

____

Cognitive Emotion Avoidance

This kind of avoidance, as the saying goes, is all in your head. These are the mental actions you use to avoid facing your anxious or depressed feelings head-on. *Cognitive emotion-avoidance* strategies can be particularly difficult for you to identify—and you may not even be aware that you're using them. *Distraction* and *suppression* are the most common cognitive emotion-avoidance strategies.

Distraction is the mental act of directing your attention away from features of your anxious or depressed experiences to avoid feeling them. You might distract yourself from depressed thoughts that you're a failure by keeping busy with small unimportant tasks. If you're anxious when driving, you might distract yourself by listening to music and singing along. Last, you might distract yourself from thoughts of a very scary event—such as losing your job—by thinking about little things that relate to that larger scary event, such as whether you'll finish a work project on time or whether your boss likes you.

Suppression is a mental act of trying *not* to think about the events that trigger your anxious or depressed feelings. You might try to push distressing memories away, such as the memory of tripping in front of a colleague at work and feeling intensely embarrassed. You might try to push away images that cause you to feel depressed or guilty, such as the image of your partner walking out the door at the end of an argument with you. You might try to push away terrifying images that you're sick or that you've hurt a loved one in some way, although you know that you have not.

Describe cognitive emotion-avoidance strategies you use to avoid feeling anxious or depressed:

____

____

____

Protective Signals

Protective signals is the final emotion-avoidance strategy. Protective signals are items that you carry with you to avoid feeling uncomfortable. They reassure you by signaling that you're safe. For example, you might carry medication or even empty medication bottles when you travel away from home or fly in a plane to avoid feeling too anxious. If you worry that a dry mouth will trigger a panic attack, you might carry a water bottle to avoid your anxious feelings. You might travel with a special blanket or doll to avoid feeling anxious. These protective signals function a bit like a talisman that you believe wards off potentially threatening or difficult experiences.

You might think that relying on these small protective signals is harmless. Afterall, with them you can engage in activities that you would otherwise avoid. However, relying on protective signals to engage in certain activities undermines your confidence that you can tolerate and manage your anxious or depressed feelings on your own, without "magical" medications, socks, or beans.

Describe the protective signals you use to feel more comfortable when you're unable to directly avoid a situation or activity:

____

____

____

____

____

____

The particular emotion-avoidance strategies a person might use depends on the person and the particular events and activities that trigger their anxious or depressed feelings. Look at the Examples of Emotion-Avoidance Actions table. How do the emotion-avoidance strategies you use compare to those Mateo, Nia, Rosario, Malik, and Janine use? At the bottom of the table, describe the emotion-avoidance actions or strategies you use to avoid triggering your anxious or depressed feelings.

Examples of Emotion-Avoidance Actions

	Situational Emotion-Avoidance Actions	Subtle Behavioral Emotion-Avoidance Actions	Cognitive Emotion-Avoidance Actions	Protective Signals
Panic disorder *(Mateo)*	Avoid escalators, stairs. Avoid running or climbing stairs. Avoid social events. Avoid driving.	Avoid walking quickly. Avoid stressful topics when speaking to colleagues.	Avoid focusing on the dizzy feelings or shortness of breath.	Carry asthma inhaler. Carry Ativan.
Generalized anxiety disorder *(Nia)*	Avoid working on my résumé or searching online for jobs. Avoid asking for a raise.	Avoid telling Pete he did or said something that upset me.	Avoid thinking about my career. Distract from my health worries.	Carry Valentine card Pete gave me last year. Carry Xanax.
Social anxiety disorder *(Rosario)*	Avoid public speaking. Avoid speaking to principal.	Avoid wearing red blouses. Avoid eye contact with people I don't know.	Avoid thinking about things I love about teaching. Avoid thinking about blushing.	Carry heavy makeup. Carry scarf to cover my neck. Carry my letter of resignation.

Obsessive-compulsive disorder *(Malik)*	Avoid public restrooms. Avoid touching anything that is red.	Keep hands in pockets in public. Cover nose and mouth with top of T-shirt. Open doors with foot or tissue.	Avoid thinking about germs or diseases.	Carry hand sanitizer, baby wipes, and rubber gloves.
Major depressive disorder *(Janine)*	Avoid social events with kids. Avoid talking about divorce with friends. Avoid doing anything that requires mental or physical effort.	Look away when I see mothers playing with their kids. Avoid talking with my kids about their dad.	Avoid thinking about the mistakes I made in the marriage.	Carry the list of good things about me that me and my therapist came up with.
My Emotion-Avoidance Actions				

Emotion-Driven Actions and Emotion Avoidance

Emotion-driven actions are the actions you take to escape anxious or depressed feelings or to lessen these feelings if you can't escape the event that triggers them. Emotion-*avoidance* actions differ from emotion-*driven* actions because *emotion-driven actions* happen *after* an event has triggered your anxious or depressed feelings, whereas *emotion-avoidance actions* happen *before* the event to avoid triggering your anxious or depressed feelings.

An example of *emotion-avoidance action* is to avoid *starting* work on your taxes because, as you record your income on the tax form, this triggers strong depressive thoughts and feelings that you're a failure or a loser. An example of an *emotion-driven action*, on the other hand, is that you start to work on your taxes and then *stop* to escape your depressed feelings.

Over time, your dependence on emotion-driven actions to escape or control your anxious and depressed feelings lessens your tolerance to these feelings. You then become even more dependent on these emotion-driven actions for relief. Furthermore—and this is the most perverse aspect of emotion-driven actions—these actions become reminders or triggers for the thoughts fueling your anxious or depressed feelings.

For example, each time you start and then stop working on your taxes, you trigger more thoughts of failure. You then respond with more emotion-driven actions that repeatedly strengthen the connection between your feelings and your emotion-driven actions. It doesn't take long for this pattern to become rigid and more frequent. Emotion-driven actions take two forms: behavioral and mental.

Behavioral Emotion-Driven Actions

Behavioral emotion-driven actions are the things that you do to control your intense anxious or depressed feelings. For example, you might endlessly work on a college application but never send it out because you're worried that anything less than "perfect" means that a potential college will reject your application and you. However, you'll never write the "perfect" application; there's always a word or phrase you could improve. In the end, there's no application, no college acceptance—you've set yourself up to feel even more depressed and anxious because you think that only a loser can't complete a college application, perfect or otherwise.

If you're intensely worried that your colleagues will think that you're incompetent, you might spend hours preparing and rehearsing a simple presentation that your colleagues might spend just ten minutes on. You might set your alarm clock extra early to avoid worrying about being late to an event, or set two alarm clocks. You might make excuses to leave a meeting early because the meeting is triggering thoughts that you're worthless or that people think you're weird.

Think back to a recent event in which you were feeling intensely anxious or depressed. Describe the specific behavioral actions that your anxious or depressed feelings motivated you to perform. Include the subtle emotion-driven actions too, such as looking away or rubbing your hands on your pants to clean them:

____

____

____

____

Mental Emotion-Driven Actions

In addition to behaviors, you might use *mental emotion-driven actions* to dampen intense anxious or depressed feelings. For example, you might repeatedly think through the various things you could have done to prevent backing into your neighbor's car, or dropping the vase of flowers, or erasing a computer file you needed for work. Or you might overfocus on what you did and said that resulted in someone (you assume) disliking you.

You might feel intensely anxious about a small ache or pain, and reassure yourself by repeating to yourself what your physician said: "You're fine." You might attempt to reason or rationalize your way out of feeling anxious or depressed. In fact, your attempts at rationalization might seem similar to the flexible thinking strategies you learned in the previous chapter. However, if you use a flexible thinking strategy to push away, escape from, or quickly dampen your anxious or depressed feelings, then it's likely an emotion-avoidance action.

Think back to a recent event in which you were feeling intensely anxious or depressed. Describe the specific mental actions you performed to control your anxious or depressed feelings:

____

____

____

____

Another mental emotion-driven action is *rumination*, a pattern whereby you dwell on difficult or upsetting events and can't stop thinking about them. Thinking about a problem is normal, and you'll typically stop thinking about it once you've resolved the problem. Rumination, on the other hand, continues because you focus on consequences and causes of a problem but not solutions to the problem. In fact, rumination gets in the way of adaptive problem solving. You'll learn more about rumination later along with flexible action strategies that focus on this mental process.

The emotion-driven actions people use depend on the person and the particular events, situations, and activities that trigger their anxious or depressed feelings. How do the emotion-driven actions you use compare to those Mateo, Nia, Rosario, Malik, and Janine use? Look at their Examples of Emotion-Driven Actions. Then, at the bottom of the chart, describe the emotion-driven actions you use to control your anxious or depressed feelings.

Examples of Emotion-Driven Actions

	Behavioral Emotion-Driven Actions	Mental Emotion-Driven Actions
Panic disorder *(Mateo)*	Lean against chairs or walls. Cut stressful conversations short.	Distract myself from dizzy feelings. Repeatedly tell myself that it's just stress.
Generalized anxiety disorder *(Nia)*	Repeatedly ask Pete if he loves me. Working and reworking résumé. Set alarm clock an hour early for meetings. Repeatedly talk with mom about my health.	Repeatedly tell myself all the nice things that Pete tells me. Distract myself when I start to worry. Push my health worries to the back of my mind.
Social anxiety disorder *(Rosario)*	Spend hours practicing a 10-minute presentation. Wear makeup to hide blushing.	Repeatedly think something positive about me when I'm worried that people think I'm incompetent.

Obsessive-compulsive disorder *(Malik)*	Repeatedly wash hands. Change clothes before entering apartment. Shake hands dry rather than drying with a hand towel.	Repeatedly tell myself that I'm clean. Replay in my mind everything I touched. Push dirty thoughts away.
Major depressive disorder *(Janine)*	Make excuses to leave social events early. Go to bed after ex-husband picks up kids. Tell friends that divorce is all my fault.	Dwell on all the bad things about my marriage. Repeatedly recite to myself the things I didn't like about my ex.
My Behavioral and Mental Emotion-Driven Actions		

Flexible Action Strategies

The following strategies will build more flexible action into your emotional responses. Perhaps the most powerful strategy to build more flexible action is approaching rather than avoiding your anxious or depressed feelings. That is, you practice starting and sustaining activities that trigger your anxious or depressed feelings. In this way, you demonstrate to yourself that you can cope with these intense feelings in a variety of situations.

For example, if you avoid speaking to people because you fear that you'll say something "wrong," then you won't learn that it's unlikely that you'll say something wrong. More important, you won't learn that you can handle the anxiety you feel about the possibility (although unlikely) that you'll say something wrong. You'll learn more about the importance of approaching rather than avoiding your emotional responses and how to do it in chapter 8.

You also can build flexible action by changing the small behavioral and mental actions you use to dampen your anxious and depressed feelings. These small changes weaken the link between the emotion-driven action and the temporary relief you feel, and help build your emotion tolerance over time.

Alternatives to Your Typical Emotion-Driven Actions

By now, you have an idea of the typical emotion-driven actions you use to avoid, escape, dampen, and control your anxious or depressed feelings. Now it's time to identify *alternative actions* to add flexibility to your emotional system. Alternative actions are counterintuitive to your feelings. However, acting counterintuitively to your feelings is the key to building emotional flexibility; it helps you learn that your feelings don't have to determine how you act. Keep in mind that it's not necessary that the alternative actions be big. In fact, even small actions, such as smiling when you feel down or looking at someone's face as you speak to them, can make a big difference when you practice them repeatedly over time.

The first step in learning to respond counterintuitively to your anxious and depressed feelings is to identify the alternative actions that you'll practice. By now, you've completed many ABCs of Emotion Worksheets. As you review them, you'll see the typical strategies you use to avoid or control your anxious or depressed feelings. For examples of alternative actions, look at those that Janine and Mateo identified.

Janine's Identify Alternative Actions Worksheet

Type of Action	Emotion-Driven Action	Alternative Action
Avoidance		
Situational	Avoid social events with kids. Avoid talking about divorce with friends. Avoid doing anything that requires mental or physical effort.	Go to parties and other activities with kids. Talk to close friends about divorce. Take a 10-minute walk every day. Read one short magazine article every day.
Subtle Behavioral	Look away when I see mothers playing with their kids. Avoid talking with my kids about their dad.	Look at mothers playing with their kids and smile at the moms I know. When my kids bring up their dad, talk with them about him.
Cognitive	Avoid thinking about all the mistakes I made in the marriage.	Walk the dog mindfully and accept that I'm not perfect.
Protective Signals	Carry the list of the good things about me that me and my therapist came up with.	Don't read the list to feel better, but use one of the mindfulness skills I learned to accept my thoughts and feelings.
Emotion-Driven		
Behavioral	Make excuses to leave social events early. Go to bed after ex picks up kids. Tell friends that divorce is all my fault.	Attend social events until several people leave. Go for a walk or take a bubble bath after ex picks up kids.
Mental	Dwell on all the bad things about my marriage. Repeatedly think about the things I didn't like about my ex.	Walk the dog in a mindful way. Practice mindfulness of the breath to observe these thoughts and feelings.

Mateo's Identify Alternative Actions Worksheet

Type of Action	Emotion-Driven Action	Alternative Action
Avoidance		
Situational	Avoid escalators and stairs. Avoid running or climbing stairs. Avoid social events. Avoid driving.	Ride a short escalator at the subway station. Run up the stairs in my house two times per day. Lunch with friend or colleague once a week. Drive around the block three times each day.
Subtle Behavioral	Avoid walking quickly. Avoid stressful topics when speaking to colleagues.	Walk quickly around my block twice a day. Speak to colleagues about stressful cases.
Cognitive	Avoid focusing on dizzy feelings or shortness of breath.	Practice mindfulness of breath and accept dizziness and breathlessness but with some distance.
Protective Signals	Carry asthma inhaler. Carry Ativan.	Leave asthma inhaler in locker during workout. Leave Ativan in desk when meeting with colleagues.
Emotion-Driven		
Behavioral	Lean against chairs or walls. Cut stressful conversations short.	When speaking with people, stand two steps away from walls or chairs. Continue stressful conversations for at least 10 minutes.
Mental	Distract myself from dizzy feelings. Repeatedly tell myself that it's just stress.	Practice mindfulness of breath to focus on dizziness and breathlessness but with some distance.

Now you try it. With the Identify Alternative Actions Worksheet, list your typical emotion-driven actions and then brainstorm a list of alternative actions. In this exercise, focus on both emotion-driven *behavioral* actions and *mental* actions. However, don't confuse the thinking strategies you learned in chapter 6 with alternative mental actions. Repeating a phrase to yourself (even if it's accurate) in order to decrease or avoid your anxious or depressed feelings is cognitive avoidance, or an emotion-driven mental action. For example, telling yourself that you're happy or calm when you're not doesn't work if your goal is to feel what you're feeling. Flexible thinking is accepting that you feel what you feel while recognizing that these thoughts are inaccurate and unhelpful.

Identify Alternative Actions Worksheet

Type of Action	Emotion-Driven Action	Alternative Action
Avoidance		
Situational		
Subtle Behavioral		
Cognitive		
Protective Signals		
Emotion-Driven		
Behavioral		
Mental		

Practice Alternative Actions

One of the best ways to build emotional flexibility is to act in opposition to your emotion-driven action tendencies. Alternative actions, such as smiling when you're angry or unhappy, can change the way you experience an emotion. When you're anxious, your emotion-driven action tendency is to avoid or to be overcautious. When you're depressed, your emotion-driven action tendency is to withdraw from people or to avoid doing things that you've enjoyed in the past.

In the next exercise, you'll practice some of the alternative actions you identified in the previous exercise. First, for examples of alternative actions, look at those that Janine and Rosario identified.

After reviewing the examples, it's your turn. Use the Alternative Action Practice Log to record situations that trigger your anxious or depressed feelings. Record the feeling and the emotion-driven avoidance or actions you used. Next, circle *Yes* each time you practice the alternative action in this or a similar situation. Also, write what happened when you tried the alternative action. It's important that you learn that good things (or rather, not bad things) can happen if you face rather than avoid your anxious or depressed feelings.

Janine's Practice Alternative Action Log

Situation	Feeling	Emotion-Driven Avoidance or Action	Alternative Action						What happened?
Kay called to invite me to lunch.	Exhausted.	Made up some excuse to not go.	Said yes but told her I could only stay for 30 minutes.						I had a nice time and ended up chatting with Kay for over an hour.
			(Yes)	Yes	Yes	Yes	Yes	Yes	
Picked up kids at school and saw a mother I know.	Depressed and guilty.	Looked away and quickly left the school yard.	Waved and smiled at the mother.						The mom smiled, waved back, and made sign to call her.
			(Yes)	(Yes)	Yes	Yes	Yes	Yes	
Awakened early, unable to go back to sleep.	Guilty and depressed.	Lay in bed thinking about my ex.	Got out of bed, danced to a couple of songs on the radio.						Got out of my head and enjoyed moving around. I haven't danced in forever.
			(Yes)	(Yes)	(Yes)	Yes	Yes	Yes	

Rosario's Practice Alternative Action Log

Situation	Feeling	Emotion-Driven Avoidance or Action	Alternative Action						What happened?
Speaking to principal at lunch.	Anxious.	Pulled up my collar to cover my neck, made an excuse to leave.	Pulled my collar down to expose my neck. Stayed until lunch ended.						The principal complimented me and asked for my opinion regarding a new district initiative.
			Yes	Yes	Yes	Yes	Yes	Yes	
Meeting with parents for parent–teacher conference.	Worried and self–conscious.	Avoided sharing my concerns for their son and only shared good things.	Shared the good things as well as my concerns about their son.						Parents told me they shared my concerns and felt good that their son has a teacher who "gets him."
			Yes	Yes	Yes	Yes	Yes	Yes	
Awakened early, unable to go back to sleep.	Worried.	Lay in bed thinking about the presentation I'm giving at the next PTA meeting.	Got out of bed, walked the dog.						Enjoyed the walk. It was a beautiful morning. It felt good not to spin in my head.
			Yes	Yes	Yes	Yes	Yes	Yes	

Practice Alternative Action Log

Situation	Feeling	Emotion-Driven Avoidance or Action	Alternative Action	What happened?
			Yes *Yes* *Yes* *Yes* *Yes* *Yes*	
			Yes *Yes* *Yes* *Yes* *Yes* *Yes*	
			Yes *Yes* *Yes* *Yes* *Yes* *Yes*	

Practice Effective Problem Solving

As you learned in chapter 2, thinking about a problem is normal and useful. It's how you develop a plan to cope with an event now and in the future. It's the way you increase the likelihood that things will turn out okay. However, intense anxiety and depression are incompatible with effective problem solving, in part because effective problem solving requires emotional flexibility. In order to solve a problem it's necessary that you're able to consider possible solutions to it: this is mental flexibility.

You can't solve all problems, but you can solve most of them, or at least you can develop a plan that lessens the impact of the problem. At the same time, in order to solve a problem, you must have some influence over the problem. For example, although you don't have much influence over whether your company goes out of business, you do have some influence over whether you want to continue working there.

At other times, you might have some influence over the problem, but it's not worth your time or energy to solve it. For example, you can contest a parking ticket and perhaps avoid paying a fine, or you might pay the ticket because it's not worth your time to go to court. If there's nothing you can or want to do to solve a problem, that's okay, but it's useless to worry or dwell on a problem that you've decided isn't worth your time to solve.

Follow these steps to solve problems effectively:

1. Identify and define the problem.

2. Brainstorm possible solutions for the problem.

3. Discard any solution that is impractical or may create more problems for you.

4. List the strengths and weaknesses of each solution.

5. Rank the effectiveness of each solution based on its strengths and weaknesses.

6. Plan and then try the best solution.

7. Review how the solution worked and decide on next steps.

Janine decided to solve rather than dwell on the problem that her friend, Alicia, isn't responding to her text messages. Janine knew that Alicia likely had stopped trying to reach her because Janine had not answered her texts in the past. Nonetheless, Janine continued to dwell on rather than solve this problem. Look at Janine's Problem Solving Worksheet to see what she decided to do and the plan she developed to carry it out.

Janine's Problem Solving Worksheet

<table>
<tr><th colspan="4">Step 1: Define Problem</th></tr>
<tr><td colspan="4">When defining the problem, try to be as clear and complete as possible. If you're having trouble separating the problem from your feelings about the problem, imagine how an impartial friend would define the problem.</td></tr>
<tr><td colspan="4">Alicia isn't returning my text messages because she's probably given up on me.</td></tr>
<tr><th colspan="4">Steps 2 and 3: Brainstorm Solutions and Examine Strengths and Weaknesses</th></tr>
<tr><td colspan="4">Write at least three possible solutions to the problem. An inflexible emotional system tends to get stuck on the same solution. There are usually several solutions to a problem, and the first or usual solution often isn't the best. Next, discard any solution that is impractical or may create more problems for you. Then, write the strengths and weakness of each of the remaining solutions. To help identify strengths and weaknesses, consider whether the solution is short term or long term, whether you'll likely follow through with the solution, and how the solution will affect other people.</td></tr>
<tr><td rowspan="3">Solution 1:</td><td colspan="2">Text my sister and ask her to ask Alicia to return my texts.</td><td rowspan="3">Rank
2</td></tr>
<tr><td>Strengths</td><td>Weaknesses</td></tr>
<tr><td>Alicia talks a lot to my sister. She'll probably listen to her.</td><td>My sister is kind of upset with me too and might not like this.</td></tr>
<tr><td rowspan="3">Solution 2:</td><td colspan="2">Go to Alicia's house and explain why I haven't returned her texts.</td><td rowspan="3">Rank
1</td></tr>
<tr><td>Strengths</td><td>Weaknesses</td></tr>
<tr><td>A face-to-face conversation means more than a text, and it's easier to explain in person.</td><td>Alicia's busy and she might not be home.</td></tr>
<tr><td rowspan="3">Solution 3:</td><td colspan="2">Send Alicia a singing telegram to apologize and ask her to text me.</td><td rowspan="3">Rank
3</td></tr>
<tr><td>Strengths</td><td>Weaknesses</td></tr>
<tr><td>It's kind of dumb, but Alicia is fun and might get a kick out of it.</td><td>It costs money. I don't know if they even have singing telegrams anymore.</td></tr>
</table>

Steps 4 and 5: Rank Effectiveness of Solution then Plan and Try Solution	
Rank the solutions 1 to 3, whereby 1 is the first solution to try. Once you select the solution to try first, then plan when, where, and how you'll implement the solution. You can schedule some solutions (for example, 4:00 p.m. Friday), or implement them when something happens (for example, when I feel frustrated, or when Jeff calls me). Next, describe how you'll do it. List the specific steps you'll take to implement the solution.	
When and Where	Saturday, 11 a.m. Alicia has yoga class and is usually home after that.
Steps	Check that yoga class is at 11 a.m., to be certain. Take kids to my sister's place for a couple of hours while I do this. Buy one of Alicia's favorite scented candles as a peace offering. Write what I want to say to Alicia and practice a few times first.

Step 6: Review How Solution Worked and Decide Next Steps
Last, after you implement the solution, review what worked and what didn't. Even if your problem was a one-time situation, you can learn something that will help solve the problem more quickly if it arises again. Take a moment to reflect on your problem and how you handled it. If the solution didn't work, think through what you might do differently next time, or try the next solution.
Alicia was a little cool at first, but she warmed up after I gave her the candle. She said she understood but was hurt because she thought we were best friends. I set up a lunch date with her and texted her when I got home to thank her again. She texted me right back.

Now you try it. Identify a problem you're dwelling on and use the Problem Solving Worksheet to solve it. Remember, in order to solve a problem, it's necessary that you have some influence over it. If you don't have any influence over the problem, then apply other strategies, such as mindfulness (see chapter 5), to practice dwelling less on the problem.

Problem Solving Worksheet

Step 1: Define Problem
When defining the problem, try to be as clear and complete as possible. If you're having trouble separating the problem from your feelings about the problem, imagine how an impartial friend would define the problem.

Steps 2 and 3: Brainstorm Solutions and Examine Strengths and Weaknesses			
Write at least three possible solutions to the problem. An inflexible emotional system tends to get stuck on the same solution. There are usually several solutions to a problem, and the first or usual solution often isn't the best. Next, discard any solution that is impractical or may create more problems for you. Then, write the strengths and weakness of each of the remaining solutions. To help identify strengths and weaknesses, consider whether the solution is short term or long term, whether you'll likely follow through with the solution, and how the solution will affect other people.			
Solution 1:			Rank
	Strengths	**Weaknesses**	
Solution 2:			Rank
	Strengths	**Weaknesses**	
Solution 3:			Rank
	Strengths	**Weaknesses**	

Steps 4 and 5: Rank Effectiveness of Solution then Plan and Try Solution	
Rank the solutions 1 to 3, whereby 1 is the first solution to try. Once you select the solution to try first, then plan when, where, and how you'll implement the solution. You can schedule some solutions (for example, 4:00 p.m. Friday), or implement them when something happens (for example, when I feel frustrated, or when Jeff calls me). Next, describe how you'll do it. List the specific steps you'll take to implement the solution.	
When and Where	
Steps	

Step 6: Review How Solution Worked and Decide Next Steps
Last, after you implement the solution, review what worked and what didn't. Even if your problem was a one-time situation, you can learn something that will help solve the problem more quickly if it arises again. Take a moment to reflect on your problem and how you handled it. If the solution didn't work, think through what you might do differently next time, or try the next solution.

Postpone Emotion-Driven Mental Actions

An inflexible emotional system makes it difficult for you to stop dwelling on or worrying about an event. In fact, you can't *stop* thinking about something, because the only way to know whether you've stopped thinking about something is to check whether you're thinking about it! And the moment you check whether you're thinking about it, you start thinking about it! However, you can learn to postpone worrying or dwelling on past negative events.

Postponing works great for occasional worrying or for the times you find that you're dwelling on a big event that's days, weeks, or even months away, such as a flight across the country or giving a speech at your best friend's wedding. In the previous section, you learned steps to solve problems. Postponing is similar, but instead of planning what you'll do to solve a problem, you decide to think about the problem and solve it later.

Follow these steps to postpone these emotion-driven mental actions:

1. Decide that you don't want to think about the event now. If you've already developed a solution to the problem, remind yourself that there's no point in thinking about the problem until you're ready to implement a plan to solve it.

2. Decide what you'll do to prepare for the event.

3. Decide when you'll start preparing for the event, down to the specific day and time. For example, you might make a to-do list and prioritize the items on the list. If there is more than one step to prepare for the event, assign a day and time you'll start each individual step.

4. When you begin to worry or dwell on the problem, remind yourself that you're postponing worrying or dwelling to the day and time you decided. Then, switch to one of the skills you've learned in the previous chapters, such as mindfulness of the breath.

5. If you're worrying about or dwelling on a decision to make, decide the day and time you'll sit down to gather information needed to make the decision, and examine the pros and cons of the various decisions you could make. You can set aside several short times each day to do this if that works better for you.

Janine decided to postpone dwelling on the telephone call she was to have with her ex-husband on Saturday. Every time she thought about speaking to him she felt guilty and depressed. Look at her Postpone Worry or Dwelling Worksheet.

Janine's Postpone Worry or Dwelling Worksheet

Instructions: Describe the event that you're worrying about or dwelling on. Try to be as specific as possible. For example, rather than "The meeting tomorrow," write "The meeting tomorrow when I present to the entire 15-member team." Next, describe what you'll do to prepare for the event. If there is more than one step to prepare, write all the steps and then schedule work on the steps in your calendar. When you start to think about the event, remind yourself that you're postponing worrying or dwelling until the day and time you selected. Then, switch to a coping strategy you've learned. For example, mindfulness of the breath.

What is the event that you're worrying about or dwelling on?
I hate talking to my ex. He's always so nice. That only makes me feel worse. I keep thinking about all the mistakes I made in the marriage and what a horrible wife and mother I am. Then, I start to remember other conversations I had with him when we were married and how terrible I felt about myself then too.
What will you do to prepare for the event?
I'll practice mindfulness of the breath before the call. Maybe it will help to imagine talking to him while I practice mindfulness. That could help. After the call, I'll walk the dog. The weather has been beautiful. I'll call Alicia and we can walk our dogs together. I always feel a little better after I spend time with Alicia.
When will you start to prepare for the event?
I'll practice mindfulness every morning and evening before the call. I'll call Alicia tomorrow to confirm a time to meet after the call with my ex.
What skills will you use to switch off the worrying or dwelling?
Mindfulness, exercise, sharing with Alicia.

Now you try it. Identify an event you're worrying about or dwelling on. Use the Postpone Worry or Dwelling Worksheet to develop a plan to delay these emotion-driven mental actions. Remember, when you postpone worrying and dwelling, you're controlling these emotion-driven mental processes. As you gain control over the process, you'll feel less anxious and down.

Postpone Worry or Dwelling Worksheet

Instructions: Describe the event that you're worrying about or dwelling on. Try to be as specific as possible. For example, rather than "The meeting tomorrow," write "The meeting tomorrow when I present to the entire 15-member team." Next, describe what you'll do to prepare for the event. If there is more than one step to prepare, write all the steps and then schedule work on the steps in your calendar. When you start to think about the event, remind yourself that you're postponing worrying or dwelling until the day and time you selected. Then, switch to a coping strategy you've learned. For example, mindfulness of the breath.

What is the event that you're worrying about or dwelling on?
What will you do to prepare for the event?
When will you start to prepare for the event?
What skills will you use to switch off the worrying or dwelling?

Postpone Emotion-Driven Mental Actions in Steps

Postponing works great for recurring worry or dwelling, such as worrying about your health or dwelling on a recent setback at work, but it can be difficult for some people. If you're struggling to postpone these emotion-driven mental actions, it might help to postpone in steps. This means that you begin with small postponing goals, perhaps just five to ten minutes several times each day, and then you increase the length you postpone by five to ten minutes every few days. Or set several times (for example, ten to twelve times) during the day specifically to worry or dwell, and postpone between these periods. As postponing gets a little easier, drop out one of the worry or dwell periods so that the period between active worrying and dwelling increases.

Nia decided to try postponing the biggest nonstop worry she has: her fear that Pete will break up with her. Although Pete tells her over and over that he loves her and isn't planning to leave, Nia can't stop worrying about this. So, she decided to postpone it. Look at Nia's Postpone Worry or Dwelling in Steps Worksheet.

Nia's Postpone Worry or Dwelling in Steps Worksheet

Date: July 7

Instructions: Select several times each day to worry or dwell on events or situations. Then, select how much time you plan to worry or dwell (set a goal of at least 10 minutes). When the worry or dwelling time arrives, give the worry or dwelling your full attention. When you begin to worry or dwell between the periods you designated, remind yourself that you'll have plenty of uninterrupted time to worry or dwell later, and then distract yourself or, better yet, practice mindfulness of the breath or engage in a mindful activity. If postponing is working well, then slowly decrease the frequency or length of the worry or dwelling time. Remember, be realistic. The average person worries 5 to 10 percent of the time. The goal of postponing is to significantly decrease the frequency, intensity, and duration of your worry or dwelling, not eliminate it.

	Time of Day (a.m. to p.m.)																		
Week	**6**	**7**	**8**	**9**	**10**	**11**	**12**	**1**	**2**	**3**	**4**	**5**	**6**	**7**	**8**	**9**	**10**	**11**	**12**
1		10 min		10 min		10 min		10 min		10 min		10 min		10 min					
2		10 min				10 min				10 min				10 min					
3		15 min					15 min					15 min							
4		15 min							15 min										
5		15 min					15 min												

Comments: Mindful activities like sewing, or walking with Pete, are the best activities for me. At lunch, I sometimes try mindfulness of the breath. I always remind myself to lean into the worries when it's time to worry. It's working!

Exercise: Postpone Emotion-Driven Mental Actions in Steps

Now you try it. Identify a problem you're worrying about or dwelling on and use the Postpone Worry or Dwelling in Steps Worksheet to develop a plan to postpone these emotion-driven mental actions. Remember, when you postpone worrying and dwelling, you're controlling these emotion-driven mental processes. As you gain control over the process, you'll feel less anxious and down.

Postpone Worry or Dwelling in Steps Worksheet

Date:

Instructions: Select several times each day to worry or dwell on events or situations. Then, select how much time you plan to worry or dwell (set a goal of at least 10 minutes). When the worry or dwelling time arrives, give the worry or dwelling your full attention. When you begin to worry or dwell between the periods you designated, remind yourself that you'll have plenty of uninterrupted time to worry or dwell later, and then distract yourself or, better yet, practice mindfulness of the breath or engage in a mindful activity. If postponing is working well, then slowly decrease the frequency or length of the worry or dwelling time. Remember, be realistic. The average person worries 5 to 10 percent of the time. The goal of postponing is to significantly decrease the frequency, intensity, and duration of your worry or dwelling, not eliminate it.

	Time of Day (a.m. to p.m.)																		
Week	6	7	8	9	10	11	12	1	2	3	4	5	6	7	8	9	10	11	12
1																			
2																			
3																			
4																			
5																			

Comments:

Change Why to How

When you're intensely anxious or depressed, your mind repeatedly dwells. For example, when you're depressed, you dwell on your mistakes (real or actual), your shortcomings, and past incidents or events, relentlessly and repeatedly asking yourself, "Why did I do that?" "Why am I such a failure?" "Why did that happened to me?" These repeated thoughts about your inadequacy or worthlessness lead to a sense of hopelessness. Once you're hopeless, you can't solve the problems in your life. You think, "What's the point?" and begin to feel powerless and overwhelmed. The depression deepens and there you sit, unable to stop these mental actions. This is *depressive rumination*.

Whereas depressive rumination is typically about the past, *anxious rumination* is about the future. When you're anxious, you dwell on the threat and on how you hope to avert the disaster, solve the problem, or prevent the mistakes you predict you'll make. For example, you might worry about an upcoming important meeting and repeatedly think about what you will say and how you will say it. You might worry about having a panic attack while on the subway and repeatedly think about how you might prevent a panic attack or what you might do if it happens.

Rumination is a normal and natural response to difficult situations or problems. It's normal and natural to think through a problem to solve it, to make sense of it, or to work through it. However, a flexible emotional system is a balance between *thinking* about the upsetting event or problem and *acting* to resolve it. In other words, thinking is useful if it guides you to act, and acting guides further thinking.

Now, imagine that your car doesn't start one morning as you're headed to work. You begin to think of the possible reasons the car isn't starting (for example, out of gas, dead battery, broken starter) and this leads you to different solutions to the problem. However, thinking without acting to solve the problem won't get the car to start. Similarly, just acting without thinking (for example, repeatedly turning the key in the ignition) isn't likely to get the car started either.

When you're ruminating, you're likely asking yourself "why" questions. "Why is this happening to me?" or "Why do these things keep happening to me?" Questions like these focus on you as the problem rather than on the car as the problem.

Describe the kinds of events on which you dwell or the repeated "why" thinking that maintains your anxious or depressed feelings.

____

____

____

____

____

Describe how these mental actions make you feel. Do you feel less anxious, depressed, angry, or guilty? Or do you feel more?

____

____

____

Describe how these mental actions influence your motivation to try new things or engage in difficult tasks. Do these mental actions increase or decrease your energy or motivation? Do these mental actions increase or decrease the likelihood that you'll develop plans and act on them?

____

____

____

In the following exercise, you'll learn to shift your mental actions from big-picture "why" thinking to small-picture "how" thinking. Janine is definitely a "why" thinker. She relentlessly asks herself questions that she can't answer, which makes her feel more depressed. "Why did my husband divorce me?" "Why am I such a lousy mom?" "Why do I continue to mess up my life?" Janine decides to practice "how" thinking. Look at her Why-to-How Thinking Worksheet.

Jeanine's Why-to-How Thinking Worksheet

Why Thinking	
Situation:	Why am I such a terrible mom?
What and How Thinking	
What is my goal or desired outcome?	
	To be a better mom to my kids.
How? What are the specific steps I'll take to achieve my goal?	
Step 1:	Make 7:00 p.m. our after-dinner playtime. We'll do this at least three times per week, and definitely on Friday and Saturday nights.
Step 2:	Buy or borrow a couple of new board games.
Step 3:	Call my mom to come to dinner on game nights to help with the little ones.
Step 4:	Buy some healthy, quick dinner foods in order to finish dinner early.
When will I do it or start to do it?	
I'll start Friday.	
Who will help me achieve my goal?	
My sister and mother.	
How did the "how" thinking work?	
The kids had a great time. Jennifer told me that she loved the new board game. I felt great about myself as a mom and slept better than I have in weeks.	

Now you try it. Identify an event that triggered your "why" thinking, and then use the Why-to-How Thinking Worksheet to shift your thinking to "how" thinking.

Why-to-How Thinking Worksheet

Why Thinking
Situation:
What and How Thinking
What is my goal or desired outcome?
How? What are the specific steps I'll take to achieve my goal?   *Step 1:*   *Step 2:*   *Step 3:*   *Step 4:*
When will I do it or start to do it?
Who will help me achieve my goal?
How did the "how" thinking work?

Long Story Short

Persistent avoidance of and attempts to control your anxious and depressed feelings is the primary reason you continue to suffer. Not only that, persistent avoidance and attempts to control your anxious and depressed feelings only intensifies these feelings when you encounter a similar event in the future. As you build flexible action, remember:

- There are two action strategies you use to avoid your feelings: you directly avoid the activities, events, and situations that trigger your anxious or depressed feelings, or you engage in emotion-driven actions to control them. Both strategies are automatic and both strategies contribute to your emotional inflexibility.
- As you practice responding counterintuitively to your anxious and depressed feelings, you'll gradually build your tolerance to these distressing emotions. Counterintuitive responses are alternative or opposite responses to your emotion tendencies.
- Emotion-driven actions include behavioral actions, such as looking away when speaking with someone, or mental actions, such as dwelling on negative events or repeatedly trying to convince yourself that you're safe.

Chapter 8

Build Emotion Tolerance

All the skills you've learned thus far are for a single purpose—to build your tolerance to your anxious or depressed feelings rather than avoid them. *Emotion exposure*, the systematic practice of engaging and interacting with your anxious and depressed feelings, is the way you'll do this. Researchers have demonstrated over many years that facing anxious or depressed feelings results in people feeling less anxious and depressed in the long run. Although it's counterintuitive, it's true.

Emotion Exposure

Emotion exposure is the process of gradually facing—rather than avoiding—the specific internal and external situations that provoke your intense anxious or depressed feelings. During emotion exposures, you'll practice the skills you've learned:

- Mindfulness, which builds flexible attention
- Thinking skills, which build flexible thinking
- Resisting avoidance and emotion-driven actions, which builds flexible action

The primary objective of these skills is to increase your willingness to face intense anxious and depressed feelings. Emotion exposure takes this a step further. Emotion exposure enables you to practice these skills in the face of intense anxious and depressed feelings. Skills that you test when you're feeling intensely anxious or down build your confidence that they work when it counts the most: when you're feeling what you're feeling in the moment. Furthermore, the more you practice these skills in the face of your intense feelings, the more automatic these skills become.

It might take two to six weeks to build this new habit of facing your anxious and depressed feelings. But with time this new habit will become second nature to you. Without thinking too much about it, you'll *automatically* resist the urge to wash your hands or to step away. In fact, with practice, you'll automatically step toward discomfort rather than avoid it. That's when things will truly change for you. This is what deep and lasting change feels like: the ability to face your feelings and master them.

What Emotion Exposure Teaches You

The goal of emotion exposure is to change an old habit you've likely developed over many years—avoiding or stepping away from your uncomfortable anxious or depressed feelings. Learning to step toward (rather than away from) your anxious or depressed feelings builds your emotion tolerance. As you build your emotion tolerance through emotion exposure, you'll learn that:

- Your anxious and depressed feelings are neither permanent nor fatal, and that they peak but always taper off, whether you try to avoid or control them or not. Once you learn this, you'll become more willing to tolerate your feelings.
- You have greater control, not less, over your anxious and depressed feelings than you believe. Your decision to step toward (rather than away from) your discomfort will help you feel less pressured, less out of control, and less down.
- You can change your old habit of avoiding uncomfortable sensations and the situations that trigger them. As you repeatedly break this old habit, your confidence increases. You'll then carry this new confidence into other situations in the future, and you'll be more likely to master those too.
- Avoidance and emotion-driven actions don't really work the way you believe they do. Nothing bad happens if you don't avoid or control your feelings. And, just as important, you learn that you can handle your feelings without any assistance—from other people or from your emotion-driven actions.

Types of Emotion Exposure

Emotion exposures take several forms. *Situation exposures* include both external and internal situations that provoke intense anxious and depressed feelings. External situations include places, objects, or activities that trigger your anxious or depressed feelings, such as sitting in a crowded room, engaging in pleasant activities, meeting new people, or touching a "dirty" object. Internal situations include thoughts, memories, or physical sensations that trigger your anxious or depressed feelings.

You'll begin with *physical sensation exposures*. These exposure exercises build your tolerance to the intense physical sensations that accompany your anxious and depressed feelings. Next, you'll practice *external situation emotion exposures*. These exposure exercises build your tolerance to the anxious and depressed feelings that arise in specific situations or when you engage in certain activities. Last, you'll practice *internal situation exposures*. These exposure exercises build your tolerance to the anxious and depressed feelings that accompany the thoughts, images, and doubts you have.

Remember, as you practice these emotion exposures, you may notice urges to avoid or control your feelings that, as you've learned, prevent you from realizing that you can cope with the full width and breadth of your uncomfortable feelings. In order to truly learn that you can handle your feelings, it's necessary that you willingly and fully experience them. No shortcuts. No one foot in and one foot out. In order to achieve greater comfort in the future, it's necessary that you learn that you can handle your feelings in the moment.

FACE Your Emotions

Before starting any of the emotion exposure exercises that follow, it's important that you first learn the correct way to practice emotion exposures. In order to FACE your emotions, follow these steps:

- **Face your anxious or depressed feelings.** Over the years, you've fallen into a habit of turning away from your anxious or depressed feelings. Turning away from these feelings means that you're not fully with these feelings as they unfold. As you repeatedly turn away from your feelings, you fail to learn that you can handle them, in their full power, in the moments you're feeling them. Learning to face your anxious or depressed feelings is essential to building your tolerance of them.

- **Anchor in the present moment.** When you practice emotion exposure, observe and accept all the parts of your anxious or depressed feelings in the present moment. Accept them without judging them, analyzing them, or suppressing them. Anchoring in the present moment means feeling what's happening now. In chapter 5, you learned and practiced skills to anchor in this way. When you're anchored in the present moment, you react less intensely to your feelings and learn more about them. From the present moment, you observe your emotions rise, crest, and decrease rather than observe what you fear: that they build and build without end. Anchoring in the present moment helps you learn that you've nothing to fear from feeling your feelings and that you can handle these feelings in their full intensity.

- **Check or resist your emotion-driven actions.** This means resisting all the subtle and not-so-subtle ways you avoid, lessen, or attempt to control your anxious or depressed feelings. Don't breathe deeply, say prayers or affirmations, space out, distract yourself, visualize positive outcomes, or do anything that takes you away from your feelings. Instead, anchor in the moment, observe your feelings, and wait for them to lessen on their own. Emotion-driven actions only get in the way of you learning that you can tolerate these intensely unpleasant feelings.

- **Endure your anxious or depressed feelings.** If you're having trouble enduring your feelings, drop down to a lower step in your emotion exposure ladder (you'll learn about the ladder later in this chapter). Or add easier steps to the ladder and start there. It's essential that you endure your anxious or depressed feelings until they decrease on their own, without trying to control these feelings in any way. If that means stepping down to an easier step on your emotion exposure ladder, then do that. It's better than escaping the feeling or trying to control it.

In addition to using FACE during each emotion exposure practice, you'll use the Emotion Exposure Planning Worksheet to set up and record what you practice and, most important, what you learn. Try to practice emotion exposure until your discomfort 50 percent or less of the maximum or peak of your distress. Tracking your emotion exposure practice in this way increases your willingness to try future practices because you learn that you can cope with these intense feelings.

Finally, to benefit fully from emotion exposure, practice repeatedly and frequently. Set aside at least thirty to forty minutes at least three to four times a week. This is quite a commitment, but with consistent and adequate practice for several weeks, your life will open again as you reverse years of avoiding and fleeing from your anxious or depressed feelings.

Now that we've learned a bit about how to practice emotion exposure in general, you'll apply emotion exposure to uncomfortable physical sensations.

Physical Sensation Exposure

At this point, you've learned the role your thoughts and actions play in your anxious and depressed feelings. Now you'll learn the role internal physical sensations play in your anxious and depressed emotional experiences. Physical sensations are part of your emotional experiences, whether you're feeling anxious or depressed. You're likely more aware of these physical sensations than you are of your thoughts or of the physical and mental emotion-driven actions that are part of your intense feelings. For that reason, your awareness of the unpleasantness of your physical sensations is likely a primary reason you've fallen into a habit of automatically avoiding or trying to control these sensations.

Furthermore, how you think about these physical sensations can intensify them. For example, as a child you might have played swinging statues. In the game, one kid holds another kid's hand and foot and swings them round and round three or four times, then lets go. When the kid who was being swung hits the ground, they stand upright and freeze into a statue, which sounds easy but it's not. While standing there, the kid's head is spinning, they may feel lightheaded or nauseous, and their heart is pounding while they try to stand perfectly still.

Now, dizziness, nausea, and a pounding heart make sense if you're playing swinging statues, but what if you're sitting in a meeting or driving your car on the freeway? What happens then? Rather than interpreting these physical sensations as fun and part of the game, you might interpret them to mean that you're dying or going crazy.

When it comes to physical sensations, it's important that you learn that these sensations aren't dangerous, overwhelming, or impossible to tolerate. That's where emotion exposures come into play. The more often you permit yourself to feel fully these physical sensations, the greater your tolerance to them builds. Furthermore, as you repeatedly practice engaging with these unpleasant physical sensations, you'll slowly break the link between these sensations and your emotion-driven actions that provide the *brief* relief that limits their emotional flexibility that contributes to your suffering.

For some people with anxiety disorders, the physical sensations are the scariest part of their anxious feelings. For example, Mateo, who has panic disorder, is terrified of the dizzy sensations he experiences in certain situations. The dizziness is a feature of Mateo's anxious feelings, along with breathing heavily and sweating. In order for Mateo to recover fully from his panic disorder, it's essential that he become less fearful of the physical sensations associated with his anxious response.

This is true for people with other anxiety disorders too. If you're afraid of spiders, you might have observed that a photo of a spider can trigger your anxious response. Of course, a photo of a spider can't bite you and therefore isn't dangerous. So what is it that you're trying to avoid—the spider or the physical sensations associated with your anxious response? As you begin to accept and tolerate these physical sensations more, you'll discover that the urge to avoid objects or situations decreases, along with the urge to avoid the distressing physical sensations that arise as part of your anxious response.

In the next exercise, you'll identify the physical sensations that are most similar to the sensations that are part of your anxious and depressed feelings. You'll focus on these physical sensations when you build your physical sensation exposure ladder—the list of specific objects or situations that trigger your anxious or depressed feelings, ranked in order of the intensity of the anxiety or depression you predict you'll feel as you face these feelings.

Exercise: Assess Your Physical Sensations

Set aside about thirty minutes for this exercise. If you're reluctant to try this alone, invite a support person to watch from a distance. Try every exercise on the list and continue the exercise for the specified time. In order to benefit from the physical sensation assessment, engage fully in each exercise. Use the blank Assess My Physical Sensations Worksheet to identify the physical sensations you'll place in your physical sensation exposure practice ladder.

At the end of each exercise, list the physical sensations (for example, breathlessness, dizziness, sweating) you noticed. Then rate the *intensity of the physical sensation* on a scale of 0 to 100 (whereby 100 is extremely intense). Next, rate the *similarity of the physical sensation* you experienced in the exercise to the physical sensation you experience when you're anxious or depressed on a 0 to 100 percent scale (whereby 100 percent means that the sensation in the exercise is identical to the physical sensation you feel when you're anxious or depressed). Last, rate the intensity of the discomfort you experienced during the exercise on a 0 to 100 scale (whereby 100 means that the physical sensation was extremely uncomfortable).

Assess My Physical Sensations Worksheet

Exercise	Physical Sensation	Sensation Intensity (0–100)	Sensation Similarity (0–100%)	Discomfort Intensity (0–100)
Shake my head from side to side for 30 seconds.				
Repeatedly (for 30 seconds) lower my head between my legs and then lift it quickly.				
Run in place for 60 seconds (check with my doctor first).				
Run in place for 60 seconds while wearing a heavy jacket.				

Exercise	Physical Sensation	Sensation Intensity (0–100)	Sensation Similarity (0–100%)	Discomfort Intensity (0–100)
Hold my breath for 60 seconds or as long as I can.				
While seated in a swivel chair (not while standing), spin for 60 seconds.				
Tense major muscles, abdomen, fists, forearms, and shoulders for 60 seconds.				
Breathe very rapidly for up to 60 seconds.				

Exercise	Physical Sensation	Sensation Intensity (0–100)	Sensation Similarity (0–100%)	Discomfort Intensity (0–100)
Breathe through a thin straw for 120 seconds.				
Stare at myself in a mirror for 90 seconds.				
Hunch my head down while frowning and tightening my jaw for 90 seconds.				
Walk with a 10-pound weight held to my abdomen for 120 seconds.				

Now, look at Mateo's Assess My Physical Sensations Worksheet. The assessment was difficult for Mateo, and he wasn't able to complete it without his wife watching from another room. Mateo noticed that some exercises didn't trigger any discomfort whereas others triggered a great deal. Furthermore, Mateo saw that dizziness was the primary physical sensation that frightened him and that the dizziness in the exercises was identical to the physical sensations he felt in certain situations that he avoided.

Mateo's Assess My Physical Sensations Worksheet

Exercise	Physical Sensation	Sensation Intensity (0–100)	Sensation Similarity (0–100%)	Discomfort Intensity (0–100)
Shake my head from side to side for 30 seconds.	Dizzy	60	90%	80
	Light-headed	50	70%	60
Repeatedly (for 30 seconds) lower my head between my legs and then lift it quickly.	Dizzy	30	20%	30
	Light-headed	30	20%	30
Run in place for 60 seconds (check with my doctor first).	Heart beating fast	80	20%	20
	Sweating	50	30%	20
	Breathless	20	30%	30
Run in place for 60 seconds while wearing a heavy jacket.	Heart beating fast	80	20%	20
	Sweating	50	30%	20
	Breathless	20	30%	30
Hold my breath for 60 seconds or as long as I can.	Light-headed	10	20%	20

Exercise	Physical Sensation	Sensation Intensity (0–100)	Sensation Similarity (0–100%)	Discomfort Intensity (0–100)
While seated in a swivel chair (not while standing), spin for 60 seconds.	Dizzy	20	20%	20
	Light-headed	20	20%	20
	Nauseous	40	50%	30
Tense major muscles, abdomen, fists, forearms, and shoulders for 60 seconds.	Muscles tingle	20	10%	0
Breathe very rapidly for up to 60 seconds.	Sweating	60	40%	30
	Dizzy	80	80%	80
	Nauseous	50	40%	40
Breathe through a thin straw for 120 seconds.	Breathless	60	30%	20
	Light-headed	70	80%	80
	Difficulty breathing	60	30%	70
Stare at myself in a mirror for 90 seconds.	See spots	20	0%	0
Hunch my head down while frowning and tightening my jaw for 90 seconds.	Neck aches	20	0%	0
Walk with a 10-pound weight held to my abdomen for 120 seconds.	Breathless	20	0%	0
	Hands feel heavy	20	0%	0

You now have an idea of the physical sensations that are the most similar to the sensations you feel when you're anxious or depressed. You also know which physical sensations make you the most uncomfortable. Now, it's time to list which physical sensation exposure exercises you'll practice.

Mateo listed the exercises to practice in the following order:

- Least intense and similar: Shaking head from side to side for 30 seconds.
- Moderately intense and similar: Spin in swivel chair.
- Most intense and similar: Breathe rapidly for 60 seconds.

Mateo decided to begin with the *shaking head from side to side* exercise. This exercise created the least intense physical sensations and were the least similar to the physical sensations he typically experiences when he's anxious. He was a bit nervous about beginning to practice these exercises but thought this activity was a good place to start.

Exercise: Practice Physical Sensation Exposure

Now, it's time to list which physical sensation exposure exercises you'll practice, based on your assessment, from the least intense and similar to the most intense and similar:

- Least intense and similar: ______________________________
- Moderately intense and similar: ______________________________
- Most intense and similar: ______________________________

If you're reluctant to practice without someone present, that's okay. Go ahead and practice the first few times with your support person. Eventually, however, practice the same exercise without your support person to get the full benefit from the exercise. As you practice the exercises alone, you'll gain confidence that you can handle the uncomfortable sensations without help from anyone. Track your progress with the Track My Physical Sensations Response Log.

Look at Mateo's Track My Physical Sensations Exposure Log to get an idea of how to record your progress.

Mateo's Track My Physical Sensations Response Log

Instructions: Every day practice the assigned physical sensation exposure task. Use one of these forms for each physical sensation. Next to the date of each practice, rate (0–100) the maximum intensity of the sensation and the maximum discomfort you feel about the sensation. Write these numbers in each of the four quadrants of the boxes. Enter the first practice in the top box and enter subsequent practices in the boxes clockwise.

Physical Sensation: Spin in swivel chair.

Absent	Mild	Moderate	Much	Maximum
0	25	50	75	100

Date	Intensity	Discomfort	Date	Intensity	Discomfort
Feb 12	40 / 35 / 40 / 35	25 / 20 / 25 / 20			
Feb 12	30 / 30 / 30 / 30	20 / 10 / 10 / 10			
Feb 12	25 / 30 / 30 / 30	10 / 10 / 10 / 5			

Track My Physical Sensations Response Log

Instructions: Every day practice the assigned physical sensation exposure task. Use one of these forms for each physical sensation. Next to the date of each practice, rate (0–100) the maximum intensity of the sensation and the maximum discomfort you feel about the sensation. Write these numbers in each of the four quadrants of the boxes. Enter the first practice in the top box and enter subsequent practices in the boxes clockwise.

Physical Sensation: ______________________________

Absent	**Mild**	**Moderate**	**Much**	**Maximum**
0	25	50	75	100

Date	Intensity	Discomfort		Date	Intensity	Discomfort

Date	Intensity	Discomfort

Date	Intensity	Discomfort

Continue to practice until your distress level for the exercise is 20 or less for at least four consecutive practice sessions. There's no way to tell how many practices it will take to reach a distress level of 20 or less, but it's best to practice as many times as you can as close together as you can. That is, rather than practicing for six times every third day or so, try to practice every day for three or four times. Experts call this mass practice, and it's more effective than spreading your practices over a week. If at any point you grow tired, you can stop—but don't stop in the middle of a practice. This just strengthens the old habit—the one you're working so hard to break—of escaping from your uncomfortable anxious or depressed feelings.

When you practice, try not to hold back. Try to produce discomfort at least in the moderate range of intensity each time you practice. The more you put into the exercise, the more you'll get out of it. After you finish the first item, move to the next higher item on your practice ladder until none of the items create much distress or anxiety for you.

External Situation Exposure

Through external situation exposure exercises you'll practice approaching and remaining in situations that trigger intense anxious or depressed feelings. You're likely avoiding these situations, such as attending parties, driving on freeways, working on your résumé, doing pleasant activities. When you permit yourself to fully engage in situation exposures while resisting emotion-driven actions or other emotion-avoidance strategies, you'll build your emotional flexibility in several important ways:

- Your automatic appraisals and interpretations of situations, physical sensations, and your emotions themselves will begin to change, often automatically. New adaptive interpretations and appraisals will begin to emerge, particularly regarding your belief that you can't handle your anxious and depressed feelings.
- Your strategies to avoid or control intense anxious and depressed feelings begin to fall away as you learn that they're unnecessary and unhelpful.
- Your anxious and depressed feelings begin to change too. When situations trigger your anxious or depressed feelings, you'll notice that they're less intense and dampen more quickly. These are signs that your emotional system is becoming more flexible.

Build an Emotion Exposure Practice Ladder

As with physical sensation exposures, the first step in practicing situation emotion exposure is to build a practice ladder. The situation practice ladder is a list of specific objects or situations—internal and external—that trigger your anxious or depressed feelings ranked in order of the intensity of how anxious or depressed you predict you'll feel.

For example, if you're afraid to drive on freeways, some stretches of freeway likely make you more anxious than others. Your freeway practice ladder might include the specific freeways (or sections of freeways) that make you anxious ranked from the section of the freeway that makes you least anxious to the most anxious if you were to drive it. Similarly, if you're depressed and finding it difficult to engage in pleasant activities, you might build a practice ladder that includes the amount of time you engage in the activity (for example, walk the dog for ten minutes).

The process of building an emotion exposure practice ladder includes four steps:

1. Select practice situations.
2. Identify emotion-driven actions to resist.
3. Identify alternative actions.
4. Rank practice situations.

Step 1: Select Practice Situations

Think about the situations that trigger your anxious or depressed feelings. Consider situations that you avoid or situations that trigger emotion-driven actions, such as checking, distracting, or seeking reassurance from others.

For example, Rosario is afraid that people will notice that she's blushing and think that she's incompetent. Therefore, she applies heavy makeup to decrease the likelihood that people will notice if she blushes. Rosario could include two or three steps on her practice ladder to apply less and less makeup, to increase the likelihood that someone might notice that she's blushing. A final somewhat over-the-top step might be for Rosario to apply makeup that makes her look as if she's blushing, again to increase the likelihood that someone might notice that she's blushing.

In the case of Janine, every time she attends a school event, she watches the other mothers, which triggers the thought that she's a terrible mom, which increases her depressed feelings. She then either avoids speaking to the other mothers or tries to steer the conversation to topics other than their children. Janine might include steps on her practice ladder to speak to mothers about their children and her children, as well as steps to compliment the mothers about their children and the things they do with their children.

Try to develop a list that covers the range of your anxious or depressed responses—situations that trigger low, moderate, and high levels of these emotions. For example, Mateo, who is afraid to drive on freeways and surface streets, listed driving long and short distances on busy and quiet streets and on certain stretches of freeways. Janine listed pleasant activities at home and work that triggered her depressed feelings, such as attending school events with her children, doing arts and crafts, and walking her dog.

Try to describe each situation in as specific and detailed a way as you can. For example, rather than "looking down from a high place," describe the situation as "looking down from a balcony while standing three feet away from the railing." Remember to design emotion exposures to both negative and positive experiences.

As in the case of Mateo, experiencing positive emotions, such as joy or calm, can trigger worry that he is not prepared for a panic attack or that he has let his guard down. As you design your practice ladder, consider whether you're avoiding pleasant activities and positive feelings because they trigger anxious or depressed feelings.

By now, you've likely recorded a variety of anxious or depressed episodes on ABCs of Emotion Worksheets. Review these worksheets and write the *antecedents* in the "Practice Situation" column of the Emotion Exposure Planning Worksheet. You'll use this worksheet in the next three steps.

As you think through possible practice situations, you may notice that there are certain variables that influence your anxious and depressed feelings. *Proximity* to an object or situation can influence the degree of your anxious or depressed feelings. For example, Mateo, who struggles with panic disorder, knows that heights tend to trigger the dizzy feelings he fears. For him, proximity to a ledge or overlook influences his anxiety. He is more anxious when standing five feet away from a balcony, for example, than he is when standing ten feet away.

The *time* you spend in a situation or near an object is another variable that can influence the intensity of your anxious or depressed feelings. Rosario, for example, who struggles with social anxiety, fears that others will notice that she is blushing and then think she is weird or incompetent. Rosario then avoids eye contact with other teachers and her principal. Rosario feels more anxious looking into her principal's face when speaking with him for five minutes than for two minutes.

The final variable that can influence your anxious or depressed feelings is the *size or degree* of something. For example, if you're afraid of dogs, you might be more anxious around a large dog than a small one. For Janine, who struggles with depression, the intensity of her depressed feelings are influenced by the degree she believes a mother is more kind, caring, or attentive to her children than Janine. Therefore, speaking with Gloria, who Janine views as a supermom, triggers more depressed feelings than speaking with Berta, who Janine views as a good mom but not a supermom.

Step 2: Identify Emotion-Driven Actions

Next, review again the ABCs of Emotion Worksheets you've completed. Identify the typical emotion-driven actions you use to avoid or control the intensity of your anxious or depressed feelings. Write these in the "Emotion-Driven Actions" column of the Emotion Exposure Planning Worksheet. Later, you'll turn these emotion-driven actions into alternative actions so that you get the most out of every emotion exposure practice. Also, don't rank the difficulty of these practice situations yet. You'll do that after you identify alternative actions in the next step.

You can look at Mateo and Janine's Emotion Exposure Planning Worksheets, which follow the blank form, to get an idea of how to do this. In the "Practice Situation" column, Mateo included items that he tended to avoid because they triggered his anxious feelings and the emotion-driven actions he used to get him through the moment. Notice what Mateo included in the "Emotion-Driven Actions" columns.

Emotion Exposure Planning Worksheet

0	25	50	75	100
No discomfort	Some discomfort	Moderate discomfort	Strong discomfort	Extreme discomfort

Rank	Practice Situation	Emotion-Driven Actions	Alternative Actions

Similarly, Janine described attending events with her children while watching other mothers interact with their children in the "Practice Situation" column. In the "Emotion-Driven Actions" column she listed several things she did or didn't do to control her depressed feelings.

Step 3: Identify Alternative Actions

In order to get the most out of every emotion exposure practice, it's essential that you resist doing any emotion-driven actions during an emotion exposure. These emotion-driven actions are likely automatic. You will fall into the pattern of avoiding or controlling your anxious or depressed feelings without even thinking about it. To help you resist emotion-driven actions, it's important to plan ahead. The best way to resist emotion-driven actions is to do an alternative action.

In this step, you'll add to the Emotion Exposure Planning Worksheets that you've started. In the "Alternative Action" column on your worksheet, add the alternative actions you'll practice during the emotion exposure. For example, when Mateo stands on the subway platform, he avoids looking down at the tracks and stays away from the edge. He even leans back a little, just in case he feels dizzy. Furthermore, he likes to stay away from other people because he fears that if he's dizzy or lightheaded, people might accidentally push him toward the edge of the platform. Mateo took these emotion-driven actions and turned them on their heads so that he could fully engage in an emotion exposure without any of his typical emotion-driven actions. Look at Mateo's alternative actions.

Similarly, Janine thought through how she could flip her typical emotion-driven actions into alternative actions that she could practice when engaged in particular emotion exposures. Look at Janine's alternative actions following Mateo's.

Mateo's Emotion Exposure Planning Worksheet

0	25	50	75	100
No discomfort	Some discomfort	Moderate discomfort	Strong discomfort	Extreme discomfort

Rank	Practice Situation	Emotion-Driven Actions	Alternative Actions
10	Ride up escalator.	Close eyes or look away. Tightly grip handrail.	Hands in pockets, away from other people, lean over handrail a little.
90	Stand on subway platform, 3 feet away from edge, looking down at tracks.	Look away, stand with back against wall as far away from tracks as possible.	Hands in pockets, away from other people, lean forward a little.
80	Stand on balcony, 1 foot away from railing, looking down.	Look away, stand with back against wall as far away from tracks as possible.	Hands in pockets, alone, lean forward a little.
70	Stand in stairwell, 1 foot from edge of step, looking down stairs.	Tightly grip handrail. Look ahead, not down.	Hands in pockets, alone, lean forward a little.
40	Drive the freeway home from work on section that dips down toward valley.	Drive in the far right lane. Look ahead, not at road.	Look far down road, away from other cars, alone.
50	Look down from 2nd floor of parking garage 1 foot away from railing.	Tightly grip handrail. Look ahead, not down.	Hands in pockets, alone, lean forward a little.
60	Stand 6 steps up ladder.	Tightly grip step above. Look ahead, not down.	Look down, hold out hands.
100	Ride down escalator.	Tightly grip handrail. Look ahead, not down.	Look down, don't hold handrail, alone.
20	Drive on surface streets in my neighborhood.	Drive below speed limit. Drive in areas with few pedestrians.	Drive speed limit in areas with pedestrians.

Janine's Emotion Exposure Planning Worksheet

0	25	50	75	100
No discomfort	Some discomfort	Moderate discomfort	Strong discomfort	Extreme discomfort

Rank	Practice Situation	Emotion-Driven Actions	Alternative Actions
90	Go to moms' group meeting.	Never attend.	Smile, say hello to 2 moms.
100	Chat with ex–husband for 5 minutes when he picks up kids.	Leave room when ex enters house.	Smile at ex and ask what he's doing for fun.
80	Speak to other homeroom mother at school.	Shorten interactions, make excuses to avoid speaking.	Speak with homeroom mom for 10 minutes, ask about her hobbies.
60	Play board game with kids.	Tell kids I'm too tired to play game, or play game but only for a few minutes.	Play full board game, then make hot cocoa for kids.
70	Morning walk with friend.	Either avoid walks with friends or pretend to be "fine" while walking.	Invite friend to walk 2 days per week, tell friend how I'm doing.
40	Scrapbook with Cindy for 2 hours.	Don't scrapbook.	Scrapbook with Cindy, make light lunch to share.
50	Walk dog alone for 30 minutes.	Usually, walk dog when I know I won't see anyone, only for a few minutes.	Walk dog in morning after I drop off kids at school, smile at people I pass.
30	Walk dog alone for 10 minutes.	Usually, walk dog when I know I won't see anyone.	Walk dog in morning after I drop off kids at school, smile at people I pass.
10	Read story to Jamie.	Usually avoid reading to Jamie, but if I do, read story quickly.	Read for 30 minutes, speak with Jamie about her favorite pictures in the book.
20	Read story to kids.	Limit it to 1 story, read it quickly.	Read 2 stories to kids, take my time, ask them to select books, ask them about pictures in the books.

Step 4: Rank Practice Situations

Now, it's time for the final step. In this step, you'll rank the situations on a 0 to 100 scale based on how anxious or depressed you predict you'll feel if you engage in the situation or activity completely without doing any emotion-driven actions to decrease your anxious or depressed feelings. If two practice situations feel as if they would be equally difficult, ask yourself which you would do first. You'll likely select the one that's a little easier. Place that below the other one on your practice ladder. In the "Rank" column, rate each situation from 0 to 100. Look at Mateo and Janine's Emotion Exposure Planning Worksheets to see how they ranked their practice situations.

Practice External Situation Emotion Exposure

Now that you've created your situation emotion exposure ladder, it's time to practice the first emotion exposure. In this section and the next, you'll apply the FACE procedure both to external situations that trigger your anxious and depressed feelings and to internal situations, such as uncomfortable thoughts and images that are part of your anxious or depressed emotions, as well as certain physical sensations that are part of these emotions.

The goal of emotion exposure, as you've learned, is to increase your emotion tolerance and thereby your emotional flexibility. Emotional flexibility increases because you learn something during an emotion exposure practice that contributes to greater flexibility in the way you think, attend, and act. Perhaps the most important change in your thinking is that you can handle your intense anxious or depressed feelings—and therefore avoidance and emotion-driven actions are unnecessary.

To help with this new learning, it's important to track:

- What you thought, felt, and did before the practice
- What you want to remember during the practice
- What you learned from the practice

Look at one of Mateo's Emotion Exposure Practice Logs. Notice how Mateo predicted that he would have a panic attack during the emotion practice and that this prediction made him feel very anxious. He also noticed that he had urges to grip the handrail tightly but countered that emotion-driven action by loosening his grip a little. Last, Mateo reflected on what he learned, which helped build his confidence and thereby his willingness to try the same emotion exposure again.

Mateo's Emotion Exposure Practice Log

Instructions: Describe the emotion exposure task from your emotion exposure practice ladder. Also describe the alternative actions you'll use during the task. Describe what you learned in the prior emotion exposure practice that was helpful. Before you begin the emotion exposure, describe what you're thinking (for example, predictions, interpretations, assumptions), the physical sensations you're feeling, and any actions or urges to control your feelings. After you complete the emotion exposure, describe the length of time (in minutes) that you engaged in the practice, how uncomfortable (0 to 10) you felt during and at the conclusion of the practice, and your attempts, if any, to control or dampen your feelings. Last, describe what you learned that was helpful. Did your feared outcome occur? Were you able to cope with the feelings, and how did you do this? Were your predictions, interpretations, or assumptions correct or incorrect?

Emotion exposure task:	Look out conference window on the 24th floor, 1 foot away from the window. Hands in pockets, away from other people, lean forward a little.
Prior Learning to Remember for This Practice	
I predicted I would have a panic attack, get dizzy, and fall, but I didn't when I tried the exposure the last time. I was anxious and did feel dizzy, but I didn't fall. I don't need to put my hands out to catch myself, and leaning forward doesn't mean I'll fall even when I'm feeling dizzy. The dizziness is part of my anxious feelings.	
Before Emotion Exposure Practice	
Rate your anticipatory discomfort (0–10):	3
What are you thinking?	I'm going to get dizzy and pass out if I feel panicky.
What physical sensations are you experiencing?	I feel light-headed, my heart is beating fast, I'm sweating.
What are you doing or having urges to do?	I catch myself leaning back a little. I want to pull my hands out of my pockets, at least halfway.

After Emotion Exposure Practice	
Length of practice (minutes)	20 minutes
Maximum discomfort during practice (0–10):	4
Discomfort at end of practice (0–10):	2
Attempts to avoid or control emotions:	I noticed that I pulled my right hand out of my pocket when I felt panicky and dizzy. It was automatic. I also shook my head to clear it and took a deep breath to prevent a panic attack.
What did you learn?	I get panicky when I start to feel dizzy. I noticed that as I did the exposure my anxiety and dizziness lessened. This tells me that the anxiety causes the dizziness. I noticed that I wanted to pull my hands out of my pockets to catch myself if I started to pass out, but I kept my hands in my pockets. I let myself feel the light-headedness and I didn't pass out. Next time, I'll do this exposure for 30 minutes rather than 20 minutes. I noticed that I felt a lot of relief at the end of 20 minutes. That tells me a longer exposure would help me learn that I can handle the feeling for even longer than 20 minutes.

Janine's Emotion Exposure Practice Log looked a bit different. Janine decided to walk her dog, Boomer, in the morning and smile at everyone she passes. Typically, she avoided smiling at people because she believed that she didn't have the energy to speak to anyone. Also, she felt guilty about doing something for herself when she had not spent much time with her kids the day before. Janine walked Boomer and smiled at people she passed. She reflected on the experience and learned that she could handle her fatigue and guilty feelings, and that she had the energy to speak with people. In fact, she discovered that she felt a bit better on walks in which she interacted with people.

Janine's Emotion Exposure Practice Log

Instructions: Describe the emotion exposure task from your emotion exposure practice ladder. Also describe the alternative actions you'll use during the task. Describe what you learned in the prior emotion exposure practice that was helpful. Before you begin the emotion exposure, describe what you're thinking (for example, predictions, interpretations, assumptions), the physical sensations you're feeling, and any actions or urges to control your feelings. After you complete the emotion exposure, describe the length of time (in minutes) that you engaged in the practice, how uncomfortable (0 to 10) you felt during and at the conclusion of the practice, and your attempts, if any, to control or dampen your feelings. Last, describe what you learned that was helpful. Did your feared outcome occur? Were you able to cope with the feelings, and how did you do this? Were your predictions, interpretations, or assumptions correct or incorrect?

Emotion exposure task:	Walk Boomer for 10 minutes in the morning and smile at everyone I pass.
Prior Learning to Remember for This Practice	
Last time I did this exposure, I saw about seven people with their dogs. Every person I smiled at smiled back, and several women stopped to chat with me. I felt much better at the end of the walk. Usually walking Boomer is a drudge, but last time I enjoyed it more and especially liked chatting with the women I met.	
Before Emotion Exposure Practice	
Rate your anticipatory discomfort (0–10):	4
What are you thinking?	I'm kind of worrying that I won't have the energy to speak to people who want to speak with me. I'm much more tired than the last time I did this.
What physical sensations are you experiencing?	Some trouble concentrating. I feel tired and a little tense.
What are you doing or having urges to do?	I'm thinking of not going this morning. I know avoiding is my MO, so I'm going to go. But I'm thinking up excuses to tell my therapist for why I bailed out.

After Emotion Exposure Practice	
Length of practice (minutes):	15 minutes
Maximum discomfort during practice (0–10):	2
Discomfort at end of practice (0–10):	1
Attempts to avoid or control emotions:	After I saw the woman I met last time, I started to feel much better, so I resisted the urge to leave.
What did you learn?	I learned again that I can handle the guilty feelings I have when I do something good or fun for myself. I also learned that even if I'm having trouble concentrating or I feel tired, I can still walk Boomer. And once I smile at someone and talk with them, I start to feel much better pretty quickly. I guess the bottom line is to tolerate the guilt I feel so that I can take care of myself. It's okay. Just because I enjoy myself doesn't make me a bad mother.

It's essential that you spend some time reflecting on and learning from every emotion exposure you complete. You'll want to pay particular attention to the ways you avoided or controlled your feelings. The latter are your typical emotion-driven actions.

Emotion Exposure Practice Log

Instructions: Describe the emotion exposure task from your emotion exposure practice ladder. Also describe the alternative actions you'll use during the task. Describe what you learned in the prior emotion exposure practice that was helpful. Before you begin the emotion exposure, describe what you're thinking (for example, predictions, interpretations, assumptions), the physical sensations you're feeling, and any actions or urges to control your feelings. After you complete the emotion exposure, describe the length of time (in minutes) that you engaged in the practice, how uncomfortable (0 to 10) you felt during and at the conclusion of the practice, and your attempts, if any, to control or dampen your feelings. Last, describe what you learned that was helpful. Did your feared outcome occur? Were you able to cope with the feelings, and how did you do this? Were your predictions, interpretations, or assumptions correct or incorrect?

Emotion exposure task:	
Prior Learning to Remember for This Practice	
Before Emotion Exposure Practice	
Rate your anticipatory discomfort (0–10):	
What are you thinking?	
What physical sensations are you experiencing?	
What are you doing or having urges to do?	

After Emotion Exposure Practice	
Length of practice (minutes):	
Maximum discomfort during practice (0–10):	
Discomfort at end of practice (0–10):	
Attempts to avoid or control emotions:	
What did you learn?	

Now, select a place on your ladder to start. You might wish to start at the least uncomfortable step or one a little more challenging. Base your selection not just on the level of anxious or depressed feelings you predict you'll feel but also on your confidence (0 to 100 percent) that you can FACE your emotional response without making any attempts to control or avoid your feelings, including distracting yourself. Next, close your eyes and turn your awareness to your anxious or depressed feelings. Anchor to your breath (chapter 5) for a few moments.

Once you've anchored to your breath, open your attention to include your anxious or depressed feelings. You're likely feeling a bit anxious as you anticipate stepping into feelings you've likely avoided for many months and perhaps years. This is normal. Now, observe your anxious or depressed feelings without judging or analyzing them. Stay with your emotions and watch them in the moment. Accept them and remind yourself that they come and go.

Internal Situation Exposure

You've already practiced physical sensation emotion exposure, which is facing the internal physical sensations that are part of your anxious or depressed feelings. However, there is another internal experience you likely avoid. These are the particular thoughts or images that tend to intensify your anxious or depressed feelings. For example, you might have noticed that you grow more anxious days and weeks before you actually encounter a situation that makes you anxious. Usually, this means that even though you're not in the situation, you're imagining being in the situation. This image triggers your anxious response and intensifies the dread as the day nears on which you'll actually enter the situation you fear.

Mateo began to worry and feel anxious each night as he imagined riding up the escalator of the subway station. Although he lay safely in bed at home, the image of the escalator loomed large in his anxious mind and grew bigger and scarier each day. Mateo tried to avoid thinking about the escalator, but trying to avoid thinking about these images only increased his distress—as he resisted the images, he found that he couldn't think about anything else.

Similarly, any time Janine thought of her ex-husband, the image of him telling her that he wanted a divorce flashed through her mind. This image caused her to feel intensely guilty and depressed, because she blamed herself for the divorce and thought that if she'd been a better spouse and mother, her husband wouldn't have left her. Therefore, any time she thought of her husband, she quickly distracted herself by watching television or binge eating cookies.

The goal of internal situation exposures, then, is to build your tolerance to the feelings that these thoughts and images trigger. As you become comfortable with certain thoughts and images, you'll begin to reverse the habit of avoiding them. Over time and with more practice, you'll notice that these distressing thoughts and images enter your mind less often and, when they do, they soon depart on their own, lost in the sea of other thoughts and images that compete for your attention.

Build an Internal Situation Emotion Exposure Ladder

Often, internal situation emotion exposures are a great way for you to warm up for real-life situation exposures. To create an emotion exposure practice ladder for images, take your situation practice ladder and create a scenario for each step.

For example, Mateo developed a scenario in which he imagined standing on the edge of the step in a stairwell and looking down to the landing below. In the scenario, he imagined feeling dizzy and light-headed as he struggled to keep his balance on the stair. He imagined that his body was trembling and that his knees were shaking as he tipped forward, feeling as if he were about to fall forward and down the stairs. Mateo created an even scarier scene in which he imagined himself actually falling down the stairs—overcome with dizziness, unable to control his body, tipping forward and tumbling down the stairs, one after another, powerless to stop.

Mateo created a ladder with six separate scenes from the least scary to most scary. Scenes lowest in distress included riding the escalator while he felt light-headed, or driving on certain stretches of freeway waiting for the dizziness to strike. Here's one of Mateo's visualization scenarios:

> *I'm on the landing in the stairwell at work. I'm stepping off the landing to the first step when the dizziness hits me. I grab for the handrail, but I'm so dizzy that I can't seem to find it. I'm terrified, and my legs and hands are trembling. I try to lean back from the edge, but the dizziness overwhelms me and I can't control my body. I feel myself beginning to tip forward. I try desperately to lean away from the step, but I'm so confused I lean forward. I begin to feel myself falling. I'm trying to stop but I can't. I feel completely out of control as I slowly tip forward. I'm in slow motion as I watch myself begin to fall. I stretch out my hands to protect myself, but the fear paralyzes me. I can't move my arms. I slowly begin to topple like a tree, slowly falling toward the steps below.*

Janine developed a scenario in which she imagined her ex-husband telling her that he is divorcing her because she's a bad spouse and mother. Janine imagined that she felt "punched in the gut" and intensely guilty and depressed. She imagined having trouble focusing and extreme heaviness in her body. She imagined the look of disgust on her ex-husband's face and how he shook his head and walked away. Janine's ladder had other steps, including steps in which she engaged in fun activities even as she felt guilty. Here's one of Janine's visualization scenarios:

> *I'm hanging out with Cindy in the living room. We're scrapbooking and having a great time. I haven't enjoyed myself this much in many months. I'm smiling and laughing. I then start to think about my kids. I think that only a horrible mother would choose to have fun when her kids have been so deeply affected by the divorce. I'm feeling intensely guilty. I keep thinking that I've ruined their lives and that it's all my fault. I know that if I had been a better spouse, my husband wouldn't have left me. It's so selfish of me to have fun with Cindy while my kids are suffering. I'm a horrible mother and a horrible person, and I deserve every bad thing that's happened to me.*

Try to include as much detail in the scene as possible. Write it as if it's happening to you now. Write it in the first person and include as many of your thoughts and feelings as you can. Include also the unpleasant physical sensations that arise and that you want to avoid. In Mateo's case, he included the dizziness but also feeling his arms and legs trembling and the sensations of tipping forward. Janine included feeling happy with a smile on her face. Write the first visualization scenario that you want to practice here:

____

____

____

____

____

____

Exercise: Practice Internal Situation Emotion Exposure

Now that you've written a visualization scenario, record it. Find a place to practice where you won't be interrupted or distracted. Close your eyes and listen to the recording. As you listen, imagine that the recorded scenario is happening now. FACE the feelings that arise the way you've learned, and resist any urges to distract yourself from the experience that the visualization is triggering. Listen to it three to four times each day, or more if you have the time. You can also read your written scenario repeatedly. Use the Emotion Exposure Practice Log to track your learning and progress.

Long Story Short

Deep and lasting change—the kind of change that transforms your life—begins by building your tolerance to your intense anxious and depressed feelings. As you build your emotion tolerance, remember:

- You can handle your anxious and depressed feelings on your own and without trying to avoid or control them with emotion-driven actions.
- You can resist your emotion-driven actions, and as you do this repeatedly your urges to avoid or control your feelings in this way become less strong.
- You have no reason to fear or dread your emotional experiences. As you become more open to these feelings, they become less central to your suffering.

Chapter 9

Build Gratitude and Self-Compassion

Gratitude and self-compassion are critical to your recovery from excessive anxiety and depression. Gratitude enhances your happiness and well-being. Self-compassion quiets the harsh inner critic that undermines your self-confidence and self-esteem—and thereby fuels your anxious and depressed feelings.

Gratitude

Gratitude is an attitude. It's an attitude that encourages you to appreciate what you *have* rather than what you *don't* have, and what you have *now* rather than something you hope will make you happier *tomorrow.* It's an attitude that challenges the belief that you can't feel satisfied until you've satisfied every need: a new car, a new experience, or a new relationship.

Gratitude is many things to many people. For some, it's a moment of wonder: a cherry blossom, a warm chocolate chip cookie. For others, it's an appreciation of little things: your partner's wacky sense of humor or a warm bed on a cold morning. Or gratitude can be as simple as counting your blessings or not taking things for granted. Regardless of what gratitude means to you, it's a powerful way to cope in and with life. There are several benefits to building a grateful attitude toward life when you're anxious or depressed:

- **Gratitude increases happiness.** People who regularly feel grateful are more likely to feel loved and cared for by their friends, family, and colleagues. It allows you to focus on the present and appreciate what you have now rather than what you don't have and think you need. It also creates positive emotions like joy, love, and contentment, which moderate negative emotions such as anxiety and depression.

- **Gratitude increases optimism.** Gratitude enables you to see the good in every situation, regardless of how bad you may think it is. This is optimism. And although it's not always easy to see the silver lining in a situation, an optimistic attitude can help you cope with challenging situations and navigate life in a more flexible and skillful way.

- **Gratitude increases well-being.** Grateful people are more in touch with their health and well-being. Grateful people are more likely to exercise and eat healthy. People who are grateful tend to live longer and are less anxious, stressed, and depressed. Grateful people cope better with life's hard knocks because they take nothing for granted.

- **Gratitude increases overall quality of life.** Although building a grateful attitude can decrease your anxious and depressed feelings, it builds so much more. Gratitude adds value to life because you appreciate the little things that make life worth living: a stroll in the sunshine, the comfort of a well-worn flannel shirt, a child's giggles, the warmth of a beloved cat or dog on your lap.
- **Gratitude increases positive relationships with others.** Gratitude can enhance and strengthen your relationships. As you express appreciations to your spouse, child, employees, or friends, they'll feel more positive toward you. Gratitude nourishes relationships and enhances warmth and trust between people. When you express gratitude toward others, they feel more comfortable expressing concerns about the relationship when they arise.

Although building an attitude of gratitude may feel odd at first, as you experience the benefits of daily gratitude it will begin to feel real. The following exercises will build gratitude and harness the benefits that accompany appreciating life's small positive moments.

Exercise: Experience Happiness Through Gratitude

Follow these steps to experience firsthand the effect gratitude can have on your happiness and well-being:

1. Rate your happiness and well-being on a 0 to 100 scale (whereby 100 is intense feelings of happiness and well-being).
2. Sit comfortably, close your eyes, and focus on the things for which you're grateful. Begin with your health and the health and safety of your friends and family. Say to yourself, "I'm grateful that I am healthy in this moment." Imagine that you're walking in a beautiful park or on your favorite trail. Appreciate that your heart is beating and that you're healthy and strong. Appreciate that your muscles are working together to carry you where you wish to go. Appreciate that you can hear the sounds of birds or the voices of loved ones, that you can feel on your skin a gentle breeze or a kiss on the check. Appreciate what you see around you. Appreciate the colors of the trees and the sky. Appreciate that your stomach is full and that you're wearing warm and comfortable clothes. Appreciate that after your walk, you'll return to a safe and dry place to live. Appreciate that you have friends and family members who love and care about you. In your mind, list all the things inside you (your heartbeat, your sight) and the things outside you (friends, family, comforts, beauty) for which you're grateful. Open yourself to the experience of happiness and well-being now as you spend a few moments with gratitude. *[Pause for twenty seconds.]*
3. Now, re-rate the intensity of your happiness and well-being on the 0 to 100 scale.

Describe how you felt as you spent time with gratitude. Did you feel a bit happier? Did you notice a sense of greater peace or well-being? What pleasant memories of past people or events came to mind? How did they make you feel? Did you feel a bit less anxious or down?

4. Now, close your eyes again and imagine that you're sitting by a stream. The water flows slowly and is dark and deep. On the surface of the stream float hundreds of leaves, spaced several feet apart. As each leaf floats by, imagine that you place one thing (from step 2) for which you're grateful on that leaf. Watch as your health drifts away on a leaf. Watch as your ability to see, hear, and smell float away. Watch as your home, your warm clothes, the food in your pantry float away. Watch as your friends and family members float away. Open yourself to the feelings that arise as you let go of the things for which you're grateful.

5. Re-rate the intensity of your happiness and well-being on the 0 to 100 scale again.

   Describe how you felt as all the things for which you're grateful floated away. Did you feel a bit sadder or anxious? Did you notice a sense of hopelessness or powerlessness? Did unpleasant memories of past people or events come to mind? How did they make you feel?

Exercise: Keep a Gratitude Journal

Perhaps the simplest way to spend time with gratitude is to keep a gratitude journal. Keeping a gratitude journal encourages you to pay attention to the good things in life that you may otherwise take for granted. Getting numb to the regular sources of goodness in our lives opens us to more anxiety and depression. Writing your thoughts has far more emotional punch than just thinking about the things for which you're grateful. Journal writing puts you in touch with your experience and creates greater meaning about life and your place in it. Follow these tips to get the most out of your gratitude journal:

- **Commit to feeling more grateful and happier.** Your wish to experience more happiness and well-being through the process of spending time with gratitude is a key element. Like most activities, your motivation to do it and benefit from it makes a big difference in the success of your gratitude journal.
- **Strive for depth rather than breadth.** Elaborate in detail while journaling. For example, rather than listing an item you're grateful for, such as "Glen called me this morning," try "Glen took time to call me. He's busy and he didn't seem rushed in the call. He said some nice things about me and how I'm doing. I'm so fortunate to have Glen in my life."
- **Focus on people more than on things.** Although you have many things in your life for which to feel grateful, it's gratitude for the people in your life (friends, children, spouse, family members) that has the greatest influence on your happiness. Each day, write down one person whom you're grateful to have in your life.
- **Include surprises.** Record events that you didn't expect, such as a random text from a friend or the rosebud that just bloomed. Surprises elicit wonder and stronger feelings of gratitude.
- **Don't make it a job.** Writing once or twice per week is more helpful than journaling every day, perhaps because rigid and excessive journaling becomes drudgery. Instead, try for a few times per week. It doesn't matter when in the day you do it, so long as you do it.

After a few weeks of keeping your gratitude journal, check in with yourself. On the lines provided, describe how you felt during the last few weeks. Did you feel a bit lighter or less anxious? Did you smile when you entered something in your journal? Did you remember similar kindnesses from others? Did it make you want to express appreciation to others? Not just friends and family members, but toward strangers on the street?

Exercise: Write Thank-You Notes

You can enhance your happiness by writing a thank-you note that expresses your enjoyment and appreciation of a person's impact on your life. It also nurtures relationships, which are a primary source of happiness. As you write the note, open yourself to feelings of appreciation and happiness. Your eyes may fill with tears as you connect with a special kindness the person extended to you.

Send the note, or better yet, deliver it and read it in person if possible, or over the phone. Make a habit of sending at least one thank-you note per month. No time to write? Then think of someone who has done something nice for you and mentally thank the individual.

Describe how you felt as you wrote several thank-you notes. Did you experience a feeling of appreciation again? As you wrote the note, did you remember other special people you wish to thank?

Exercise: Meditate on Gratitude

Another way to spend time with gratitude is to make a gratitude meditation and listen to it daily. Gratitude happens in the present moment, and meditation involves focusing on the present moment without judgment (see chapter 5). Although people often focus on a word or phrase (such as "peace"), it's also possible to focus on what you're grateful for (for example, the smile of your child, a favorite song, the embrace of a loved one).

To begin, find a safe, quiet place where no one is likely to disturb you. Sit or lie down on your back. Make sure you're warm enough. Loosen any restrictive clothing so that you can breathe comfortably. You may wish to read the script aloud and record it so that you can play the recording while you meditate on gratitude. Try to make a recording that's about ten minutes long.

Close your eyes and take a slow, deep breath to bring yourself to the present moment and begin the process of feeling more peaceful and centered. Breathe into the belly so it expands as you breathe in and gets smaller as you breathe out.

Now, take a minute or two to mentally scan your body for any areas where there is tightness, tension, or soreness. Now, breathe your warm, oxygen-filled breath into that area. As you breathe out, release the tension.

Notice any anxiety or sadness or other feelings, such as irritation, jealousy, or guilt. Just breathe into those emotions, noting them, and allowing them to flow out as you slowly exhale.

[Pause for 30 seconds.]

Now, with a calm body and clear mind, focus on the events, experiences, people, pets, or possessions for which you feel grateful. Recall these special gifts:

- **The gift of life itself,** *the most precious gift: someone gave birth to you; someone fed you as an infant, changed your diaper, clothed you, bathed you, taught you to speak and to understand*
- **The gift of hearing,** *so that you can hear and learn: whether it's the song of a bird, the notes of an orchestra, the voices of family and friends, the sound of your own breath flowing in and flowing out*
- **The gift of a heartbeat:** *steady, regular; moment after moment pumping fresh, life-giving blood to all your organs*

[Pause for 30 seconds.]

Now, think about all the things we have today that make our life easier and more comfortable than life was for our great-great-grandparents:

- *You flip a switch, and light appears.*
- *You turn a tap and clean, drinkable water flows.*

- *You adjust a thermostat, and a room grows warmer or cooler.*
- *You have a roof to keep you dry when it rains, walls to keep out the cold wind, windows to let in the light, screens to keep out insects.*
- *You enter a vehicle and it takes you where you wish to go.*
- *You have access to machines that wash your clothes. And you have clothes to wear and places to store them.*
- *There are machines that store your food at the right temperature and help you cook it.*
- *You have indoor plumbing.*
- *You have public libraries with thousands of books, free for anyone to borrow and read.*
- *You have public schools where you learned to read and write, skills that were available to very few just a few hundred years ago.*

[Pause for 30 seconds.]

Now, take a moment to reflect on all the thousands of people who have worked hard, some without knowing you at all, to make your life easier or more pleasant:

- *People who plant, grow, and harvest your food.*
- *People who transport that food to the market.*
- *People who make the roads and railways easier to transport the food.*
- *People who maintain those vehicles, along with the drivers, loaders, and unloaders.*
- *People who designed the store, the shelves, the packaging that keeps the food safe and allows you to find what you want.*
- *Postal workers who sort the mail, others who deliver it.*
- *People who maintain the servers so you can get and send email and access the Internet.*
- *People who gather, sort, and dispose of trash and recycling to keep your home and communities clean and safe.*
- *People who gather news stories and photos to keep you informed and amused.*
- *People who play sports or create art or music that entertain and enrich you.*

[Pause for 30 seconds.]

Now, consider the people and pets you know who enrich your life. Those who smile at you and cheer you on. Those family, friends, acquaintances, colleagues, and peers. Those ancestors who worked so you could live well. Those friends who support you when you need a shoulder to cry on or a helping hand.

[Pause for 30 seconds.]

Now, take a moment to reflect on your own reasons for feeling grateful in this moment. There is so much to feel grateful for in this moment now. Gratitude fills your heart and mind, uplifting your spirit.

[Pause for 30 seconds.]

When you finish, rest quietly for several minutes, noticing how you feel throughout your body, noticing your emotions and thoughts compared with before you started. No judging, just noticing. Gently stretch your hands and arms, feet and legs. If you choose to stand, do so slowly.

On the lines provided, describe how you felt as you listened to the gratitude meditation. Did you experience feelings of happiness, peace, a sense of well-being? Did you feel less worried and anxious? Did you feel a bit more hopeful about your future and a little less down?

____

____

____

____

____

____

To summarize, gratitude isn't just about being thankful for the good things in your life; it's about being thankful for everything in your life. There are things in your life that might initially seem bad but, upon further reflection, actually give you an opportunity to learn and grow. For example, a good but not stellar job evaluation can motivate you to take on new tasks or try a little harder the next year. Part of gratitude is recognizing these blessings in all things: the ups and downs, the successes and the failures.

Self-Criticism

You, like everyone else, have an "inner voice" that talks to you. And sometimes that inner voice is quite critical. If you're anxious, you might criticize yourself for avoiding something. Mateo, who avoids riding escalators, calls himself "a wimp" or "a coward." If you try something new and fail, you might criticize yourself for that too. Self-criticism lowers your self-confidence, and lower self-confidence increases your anxiety. Your critical inner voice echoes in your head: "I'm a disaster," "I can't do anything right," "I'm weak," "I'm incompetent."

If you're depressed, you might put yourself down. Janine, amplifying the most trivial mistake, has a critical inner voice that chants, "I'm a horrible mom." "I can't do anything right." "I'm a total loser." Your self-critical inner voice counts and recounts your flaws and frailties until you believe that you're worthless, ugly, and unlovable.

Exercise: Meet Your Critical Mind

Your self-critical inner voice is so familiar that you likely don't even hear it. When you're feeling bad about something, think about what you've just said to yourself. Try to be as accurate as possible, noting your inner speech verbatim. What words do you actually use when you're self-critical? Are there key phrases that come up over and over again? What is the tone of your voice—harsh, cold, angry? Does the voice remind you of anyone in your past who was critical of you?

It's important that you get to know the tone and content of your inner self-critic, and that you become aware of when your inner judge is active. For instance, if you've just eaten half a box of cookies, does your inner voice say something like "You're disgusting," "You make me sick," and so on? Really try to get a clear sense of how you talk to yourself. Describe the tone and content of your inner self-critic:

____

____

____

____

____

____

Practice this exercise over several weeks. It will take some time to become aware of the particular ways your inner critic beats you down.

Self-Compassion

Self-compassion is treating yourself the way you would treat a friend who is struggling, even if the friend made a big mistake. Through self-compassion you become an ally rather than an adversary to yourself. Through self-compassion you replace that self-critical voice in your mind with a kind, supportive, and caring voice. Self-compassion is the antidote to the inner critic that aggravates your anxiety and sadness, your guilt and your shame. Self-compassion includes three elements: *self-kindness*, *common humanity*, and *mindfulness*.

Self-Kindness

When you make a mistake or experience a setback in life, your critical mind beats you down rather than lifts you up. Self-kindness counters your mind's self-critical tendency so that you can be as caring toward yourself as you are toward other people. Instead of criticizing or berating yourself for mistakes or missteps, self-kindness offers warmth, comfort, and caring. Self-kindness soothes the hurts that your self-critical mind inflicts.

Describe a recent setback or mistake you made. What was your critical inner voice saying about you? How did you feel about yourself in that moment? Did you believe what your critical inner voice was saying about you?

____

____

____

Now, write several kind, understanding words of comfort regarding the setback or mistake. Use words with a gentle, reassuring tone that send the message that you care about yourself.

____

____

____

Common Humanity

You're not the only human being who has failed, faltered, or considered oneself inadequate or stupid. All human beings are flawed, imperfect creatures. Common humanity links your experiences to the experiences of all humanity. Common humanity reminds you that you cannot avoid suffering and that all people suffer. It's easy to forget this when you're deep into your own suffering. Remember, setbacks are inevitable and life doesn't always proceed the way you think it "should."

Reflect on the suffering your friends, family members, and neighbors have experienced. Describe their setbacks, failures, or mistakes. How do you feel about them as you consider that they're flawed human beings? Are you critical or compassionate?

____

____

____

Now, describe the way your experience is connected to the larger human experience. You might acknowledge that being human means being imperfect, and that all people have all sorts of painful experiences. For example, if you lost your temper with a friend, remind yourself that "Everyone overreacts sometimes. It's only human." Also, describe the factors or conditions that influenced the painful event. For example, "I hated myself when I was frustrated with the kids. If I had slept better the night before, I probably would have been calmer. I'm not a perfect mom, but I'm not the worst mom in the world either."

____

____

____

Mindfulness

Through mindfulness (chapter 5) you become aware of the painful emotions that rise from self-judgment or difficult circumstances. Mindfulness means being open to the present moment in a clear and balanced manner, allowing all thoughts, emotions, and sensations to enter awareness without resisting or avoiding them. Mindfulness enables you to accept pain rather than flee from it. Accepting the pain paradoxically lessens your suffering, and mindful self-awareness enables you to experience this paradox.

Describe a recent situation in which your self-critical inner voice yelled at you loud and long. How did you feel—sad, ashamed, frightened, stressed? What did you do to try to quiet it? Did it work?

____

____

____

Now, try to accept that experience and the feelings that accompanied it. Do not judge or belittle your experience. How did your experience change? Did your feelings change? Which feelings changed the most? What was the most difficult part of accepting your experience in the moment?

____

____

____

Barriers to Self-Compassion

You've likely felt anxious or depressed for many years and have perhaps grown accustomed to your critical inner voice. You might even wonder whether it's wise to counter the familiar (self-criticism) with the unfamiliar (self-compassion). In fact, you might believe there are downsides to being kind to yourself. Suspicions or doubts about the benefits of self-compassion can make it difficult for you to build a self-compassionate attitude.

Write any doubts, concerns, or fears that you have about learning to be kinder to yourself. What are the possible downsides for you?

____

____

____

If you're like most people, you likely described one or more common misunderstandings about self-compassion that make it difficult for you to be open to practicing it. Let's look at what self-compassion is *not*:

- **Self-compassion is *not* self-pity.** Some people believe that self-compassion gives them permission to wallow in self-pity. However, self-compassion isn't just about *your* suffering. It's about *all* suffering. Self-compassion recognizes that life is hard for everyone and thereby offers some perspective on your own suffering. Rather than encouraging you to overfocus on your problems (ruminate), self-compassion enables you to step back and see your problems as part of the bigger picture of human suffering.

- **Self-compassion is *not* dangerous.** Some people are afraid to be self-compassionate because they believe that self-compassion lowers their guard. They view self-compassion as a weakness that makes them more vulnerable to hurt and unfortunate events. However, self-compassion fosters courage and enhances resilience because self-compassion builds self-confidence rather than tears it down. Self-compassionate people are better able to cope with life's tough bumps, such as divorce, chronic pain, or the loss of a job because they believe that they can weather and overcome adversity.

- **Self-compassion is *not* selfish.** Some people believe that being kind and caring toward oneself is a selfish and self-centered act. Self-criticism, they believe, drives them to be attentive and caring toward others. They worry that if they're compassionate toward themselves, then their relationships and other people will suffer. However, self-compassion enables you to give more to others because you've taken care of yourself too. A self-compassionate self is more open to caring, compromise, and stability—and these nurture relationships.
- **Self-compassion is *not* an excuse to continue bad behavior.** Some people believe that their critical inner voice keeps them on the straight and narrow. They fear that the moment they're kind rather than critical of themselves, they're headed down the slippery slope of becoming a horrible person. However, self-compassion tends to result in people taking greater responsibility for their actions, not less. Self-compassion enables you to see your mistakes, learn from them, and apologize for them.
- **Self-compassion will *not* make you lazy.** Self-compassion isn't the same as self-indulgence. You might fear that if you're kind to yourself the more likely you are to eat too much or exercise too little. In fact, self-compassion encourages you to focus on long-term health and well-being rather than the quick fix. For example, if you're trying to lose a few pounds and then harshly criticize yourself for enjoying a scoop of ice cream, you're more likely to give up and eat the entire carton. Afterall, according to your critical inner voice, that single scoop of ice cream means that you're fat, ugly, and a failure.
- **Self-compassion is *not* a barrier to achieving and getting what you want from life.** Many people believe that their harsh inner voice motivates them to work hard and achieve what they desire from life. However, the opposite is true. Self-criticism undermines self-confidence and results in more anxiety and more fear of failure. Furthermore, self-criticism builds in your mind a history of chronic failure, because no matter what you accomplish the inner critic tells you that you should have accomplished more. Soon, you're feeling hopeless and depressed, unmotivated, and having trouble getting up in the morning. Self-compassion, on the other hand, encourages you to work hard to reach your full potential, not because you *have to* but because you *want to.* This means you're less afraid to fail and have the resilience to persevere in the face of the inevitable bumps along the way.

Describe your barriers to self-compassion. Which of the above barriers do you share? Describe any doubts, concerns, or fears that you have about self-compassion that are different from the ones mentioned.

____

____

____

____

____

____

Exercise: Meet Your Compassionate Mind

Just because your self-critical inner voice is familiar doesn't mean that you can't learn to replace it with a healthy dose of self-compassion. Follow these steps to meet your self-compassionate mind and experience its soothing benefits:

1. Think about a time when a close friend felt very bad about themselves or was struggling with a setback or difficulty in life. How did you respond to your friend in this situation (especially when you're at your best). What did you say? What was your tone? How did your friend respond to you?
2. Now, think about times when you felt bad or upset with yourself or were struggling with a problem. How did you talk to *yourself* in this situation? What did you say and what was the tone you used with yourself? How did you feel and what did you then want to do?

To help organize your self-compassionate responses, reflect on the three elements of self-compassion. Then complete the Meet My Self-Compassionate Mind Worksheet. Following the blank worksheet, look at Janine's worksheet and the compassionate self-talk she developed.

Meet My Self-Compassionate Mind Worksheet

Situation	Critical Self-Talk	Feelings	Compassionate Self-Talk		
			Self-Kindness	Common Humanity	Mindfulness

Janine's Meet My Self-Compassionate Mind Worksheet

Situation	Critical Self-Talk	Feelings	Compassionate Self-Talk		
			Self-Kindness	Common Humanity	Mindfulness
After I put my kids to bed, I started to organize some photos. I saw photos of all of us before the divorce. I started to feel lonely and ate an entire bag of cookies.	I'm disgusting and ugly. No one could love me. I deserve everything that's happened to me.	Ashamed. Guilty. Depressed.	I know you ate that bag of cookies because you're feeling very sad right now. You thought a treat would cheer you up. But you feel even worse now and you hate yourself and your body. I want you to feel better and like yourself. You're still okay. Why don't you take a walk? You'll feel better soon.	Everyone has moments of sadness, and everyone copes in the best way they can. No one is perfect. Yes, eating the cookies was a mistake, but we all make mistakes and learn from them.	I accept that I feel very bad in this moment. I accept that I don't like myself in this moment. I wish I hadn't binged on the cookies, but I'm open to my pain. I do not judge it or myself for feeling what I'm feeling in this moment.

While engaging in this compassionate self-talk exercise, quietly repeat to yourself the compassionate self-talk you developed and gently stroke your arm or give yourself a hug. Physical gestures of warmth and caring can tap into self-compassion, even if you're having trouble connecting with feelings of kindness and caring. The important thing is to *act* kindly toward yourself even if you're not feeling that way in the moment. Feelings of warmth and caring will follow.

On the lines provided, describe your experience. Did you notice a difference in how you felt once you shifted into compassionate self-talk? If so, why? Which of the three elements of self-compassion (self-kindness, common humanity, and mindfulness) was the easiest, and which was the most difficult for you to practice? Please write how things might change for you if you responded to your suffering in the same way you typically respond to a close friend.

____

____

____

____

____

____

Exercise: Write a Compassionate Letter to Yourself

Over the years, you've been sending yourself one critical and mean-spirited letter after another. The letters are likely all the same. They dwell on your perceived shortcomings and mistakes. If these are the only letters you receive, it doesn't take long for you to start feeling bad about yourself and anxious or hopeless about your future. You can change this, though. The post office can deliver a compassionate letter to you as easily as it can deliver a critical one. When you're upset, struggling, or wanting to make a change that frightens you, sit down and write a compassionate letter to yourself.

Here are three ways to write a compassionate letter to yourself:

- Write a letter as if you're talking to a beloved friend who is struggling with the same concerns or issues as you.
- Write a letter as if you're writing from the perspective of an imaginary friend who is wise, loving, kind, and accepting.
- Write a letter from the compassionate part of yourself to the part of yourself that's struggling.

Place the letter in a safe place and periodically read it to yourself, particularly when you're struggling. As you read it, accept the soothing comfort that words of compassion create. At first, it may seem strange to write to yourself in a compassionate voice, but the more letters you write and the more times you read them, the easier it becomes to express compassion toward yourself.

____

____

____

____

____

____

Here's the compassionate letter Janine wrote to herself after a difficult night alone. Janine wrote from the perspective of cherished Great-Aunt Nancy, who took care of her as a child.

> Dear Janine,
>
> I know today was hard for you. Once the kids were in bed and you sat alone on the sofa, the feelings of loneliness overwhelmed you. Loneliness hits all of us from time to time, but it's particularly hard for you because you love people. The divorce changed many things, as it does for all people who go through it, but the changes are temporary. Better times are ahead, I promise you.
>
> You may not believe me, but I felt terribly lonely after your great-uncle passed away. It was a difficult year for me, and I too didn't think that I would ever feel better, but I did after a time. I accepted my sadness and loneliness, and reminded myself that although I felt alone, I was surrounded by friends and family members who loved and cared about me. I love and care about you, Janine, and with time these feelings will pass. Just give yourself some time.

Exercise: Hand on Heart

Touch is a powerful experience that not only soothes us but also enhances feelings of love, kindness, and caring. Practice this exercise any time you feel upset or ill at ease, or when you wish to step away from your anxiety, depression, or other emotional reactions while you wait for the feelings to pass. You can easily create a moment of self-compassion with these simple steps:

1. Place one hand gently over your heart. Feel its warmth on your chest. Take a moment to acknowledge the simple act of giving a calm, comforting presence to yourself.
2. Breathe slowly, gently, and deeply into the space around your heart. Feel the warmth of your hand sink deeper and expand into your body.
3. Think of a specific time when you felt safe, loved, and cherished by another person. The wonderful moment may be a memory of a time with your spouse, a parent, your child, a friend, therapist, teacher, or pet.
4. As you remember this moment, let the warmth and good feelings wash through you. You might notice your muscles relaxing or a sigh escaping. A smile might come to the corners of your mouth. Just bathe in this warm feeling of acceptance and caring. Stay in this warm memory for 30 seconds.
5. When you're ready, bring your awareness back to the room or setting. Think about any shifts you felt in your body during this practice. Carry this sense of calm and ease into your day.

Describe how you felt as you practiced the Hand on Heart exercise. Did you experience feelings of caring, kindness, and compassion? Did you feel your body relax and open to your feelings? Did you feel less anxious, stressed, or down? Describe your experience and the feelings that came up for you.

____

____

____

____

____

____

Exercise: Meditate on Loving-Kindness

Focusing on kindness and goodwill toward others can help you feel better about yourself. When practiced daily for fifteen minutes, this compassion-based meditation can lift your spirits, boost your mood, and alleviate the anxiety and stress that build over the course of a day. You may wish to read the following script aloud into a recording device. You can then listen to the recording with your eyes closed.

Become comfortable in your chair or cushion, sitting upright with your shoulders relaxed.

[Pause for 5 seconds.]

Allow your hands to rest comfortably in your lap. Gently close your eyes.

[Pause for 10 seconds.]

Settle into awareness of the body and the breath. Feeling into your body right now...noticing what's here. Open to whatever is to be experienced in the body in this moment. Connecting to the breath...noticing the wave-like movements of the belly.

[Pause 10 seconds.]

In this meditation, we'll cultivate loving-kindness. We all have within us this natural capacity for loving-kindness or friendship that is unconditional and open...gentle...supportive.

Loving-kindness is a natural opening of a compassionate heart...to ourselves and to others. It's a wish that everyone be happy. We begin with developing loving-kindness toward ourselves, allowing our hearts to open with tenderness.

Now, allow yourself to remember and open up to your basic goodness. You might remember times when you've been kind or generous. You might recall your natural desire to be happy and not to suffer. If acknowledging your own goodness is difficult, look at yourself through the eyes of someone who loves you. What does that person love about you? Or recall the unconditional love you felt from a beloved pet.

[Pause for 20 seconds.]

If it allows tender feelings of kindness to flow more easily, imagine yourself as a young child of perhaps four or five years old standing before you. As you experience this love, notice how you feel in your body. Maybe you feel some warmth in the face. Perhaps you notice a smile forming or a sense of expansiveness. This is loving-kindness, a natural feeling that is accessible to all of us, always. Rest with this feeling of open, unconditional love for a few moments.

[Pause for 20 seconds.]

Let yourself bask in the energy of loving-kindness. Breathe it in and breathe it out as you invite feelings of peace and acceptance.

[Pause for 20 seconds.]

Begin now to wish yourself well by extending words of loving-kindness to yourself.

Use the phrases offered here, or alter these phrases and choose whatever words express your wishes of loving-kindness toward yourself and others. And now, offering these words in your mind for yourself:

May I be filled with loving-kindness.

May I be held in loving-kindness.

May I feel connected and calm.

May I accept myself just as I am.

May I be happy.

May I know the natural joy of being alive.

And, now repeating in the mind these words of friendship and kindness to yourself once again:

May I be filled with loving-kindness.

May I be held in loving-kindness.

May I feel connected and calm.

May I accept myself just as I am.

May I be happy.

May I know the natural joy of being alive.

Now, open the circle of loving-kindness by bringing to mind someone who is dear to you. Someone about whom you care and who has always been supportive. Reflect on this person's basic goodness, sensing what it is in particular that you love about this person. In your heart feel your appreciation for this dear one, and begin your simple offering:

May you be filled with loving-kindness.

May you be held in loving-kindness.

May you feel my love now.

May you accept yourself just as you are.

May you be happy.

May you know the natural joy of being alive.

Now, bring to mind a "neutral" person. This is someone you might see regularly but don't know well. It might be a neighbor or a grocery store clerk. Bring this person to mind now, and repeat the words of loving-kindness:

May you be filled with loving-kindness.

May you be held in loving-kindness.

May you feel my love now.

May you accept yourself just as you are.

May you be happy.

May you know the natural joy of being alive.

And now, if it's possible for you, bring to mind someone with whom you've had a difficult relationship. Perhaps it's someone you don't like and for whom it's difficult for you to feel sympathy or compassion. See if it's possible to let go of feelings of resentment and dislike for this person. Remind yourself to see this person as a whole being, deserving of love and kindness, and as someone who feels pain and anxiety, as someone who also suffers. See if it's possible to extend to this person the words of loving-kindness in your mind:

May you be filled with loving-kindness.

May you be held in loving-kindness.

May you feel my love now.

May you accept yourself just as you are.

May you be happy.

May you know the natural joy of being alive.

Now, allow your awareness to open out in all directions, to yourself, a dear one, a neutral person, and a difficult person. Open to all beings, humans and animals living everywhere. Living in richness, poverty, war, peace, hunger, abundance. Aware of all the joys and sorrows that all beings experience:

May all beings be filled with loving-kindness.

May all beings be held in loving-kindness.

May all beings feel my love now.

May all beings accept themselves just as they are.

May all beings be happy.

May all beings know the natural joy of being alive.

And now, bring this practice to a close by coming back to extend kindness to yourself. Sit for a while and bask in the energy of loving-kindness that may have been generated here.

Describe how you meditated on loving-kindness. Were you surprised by the people you recalled who connected you to feelings of loving-kindness? What part of the exercise was the most difficult for you? What part of the exercise was the easiest for you? Did you feel more accepting and forgiving of yourself and others? Did you feel less anxious, ashamed, guilty, or down?

Exercise: Keep a Self-Compassion Journal

Try keeping a self-compassion journal for one week (or longer if you like). Journaling is an effective way to express emotions and can enhance both mental and physical well-being. At some point during the evening, when you have a few quiet moments, review the day's events. In your journal, write down anything that you felt bad about, anything you judged yourself for, or any difficult experience that caused you pain. For instance, perhaps you were angry at a waitress at lunch because she took forever to bring the check. You made a rude comment and stormed off without leaving a tip. Afterward, you felt ashamed and embarrassed. For each event, use mindfulness, a sense of common humanity, and kindness to process the event in a self-compassionate way, and add these soothing words to the journal entry.

Afterward, describe how you felt as you kept a self-compassion journal for a few days. What situations arose that triggered your self-critical inner voice? How did these harsh judgments cause you to feel?

Describe how you felt when you moved into self-compassion. Did you feel your body relax? Did you feel more accepting and forgiving of yourself? Did you feel less anxious, ashamed, guilty, or down?

___

___

___

Exercise: Take a Self-Compassion Break

Even with a great deal of self-compassion practice, your anxious or depressed mind will fall into self-criticism. It helps to give yourself quick self-compassion breaks throughout the day in addition to your daily loving-kindness meditation. A self-compassion break includes the same three components: mindfulness, common humanity, and kindness toward yourself. Follow these steps to give yourself a break from your self-critical mind:

1. **Reflect:** Think of a difficult situation that arose in your life recently that is causing you stress. Call the situation to mind, and open yourself to feelings of anxiety, stress, depression, or any emotional discomfort in your body.
2. **Mindfulness:** Say to yourself, "This is a moment of suffering." If this phrase doesn't feel right, try one of these: "This hurts," "Ouch," or "This is anxiety, depression, or stress."
3. **Common humanity:** Say to yourself, "Suffering is a part of life." Or try, "Other people feel this way," "I'm not alone," or "We all struggle in our lives."
4. **Kindness toward yourself:** Place your hands over your heart; feel the warmth and the gentle touch of your hands on your chest. If another type of soothing touch feels right to you, use that touch. Say to yourself, "May I be kind to myself."

If there is another phrase that speaks to you in your particular situation, say that to yourself instead, such as:

- *May I give myself the compassion that I deserve.*
- *May I learn to accept myself as I am.*
- *May I forgive myself.*
- *May I be strong.*
- *May I be patient.*

You can also ask yourself, "What do I need to hear right now to express kindness to myself?"

Describe how you felt during the self-compassion break. Did you feel your body relax? Did you feel more accepting or forgiving of yourself? Did you feel greater patience arise? Did you feel yourself turn away from self-criticism and toward self-acceptance? What effect did this self-compassion break have on your anxious and depressed feelings, or on other feelings you were experiencing in that moment?

____

____

____

____

____

____

Long Story Short

A grateful attitude and a compassionate self are vital to your recovery from anxiety and depression. Feeling less anxious or depressed is not the same as feeling happy. Happiness adds value to your life and makes life worth living, and gratitude is the source of this. Compassion, particularly self-compassion, is a powerful antidote to rumination: that relentless self-critical inner voice that adds to your anxious and depressed feelings. As you build a grateful and self-compassionate attitude, remember:

- Gratitude emerges in the present moment. Gratefulness for what you have now rather than striving for the next thing enhances happiness.
- It's easier to show compassion for someone you like than for someone you dislike. As you build a compassionate self, you'll begin to like yourself more. A strong and vital positive self-esteem protects you against life's bumps.
- Skills that build gratitude and self-compassion complement the skills you've learned to manage your anxious and depressed feelings. Gratitude and self-compassion inoculate you against the negative effects of a highly self-critical inner voice.

Chapter 10

Keep Going

Now that your emotional system is more flexible, you're likely feeling less anxious and depressed. That's great news! You've worked hard to build a more flexible emotional system. However, this doesn't mean that you'll never feel the pull of that old inflexible pattern of attending, thinking, and acting that intensified your excessive anxious and depressed feelings in the past. You will. That's why it's essential that you have a plan that helps you quickly get back on track.

Often, excessive anxiety and depression are barriers to achieving important life goals. Now that you're feeling less anxious and depressed, it's time to revisit the personal values that started you on the path to recovery and use them to chart your path to a fuller life.

Self-Test: Depression, Anxiety, and Stress

You've completed the workbook and now it's time to check how far you've come. Please retake the Self-Test that you've already taken twice: when you began the workbook and again midway through it. Now, compare the scores on this self-test to the two others you completed. How did you do?

Remember, building emotional flexibility takes time. You might not see a big change between the first self-test you completed and this one. That's okay. Deep emotional change comes with practice. The more you practice the skills in this workbook, the greater the change you can expect.

Respond in the Moment

In this workbook, you've learned a number of skills to break the inflexible patterns that intensify and maintain your anxious and depressed feelings. However, at this point, these patterns are weakened but not eliminated. In fact, you'll always be susceptible to slipping back into the old inflexible patterns of attending, thinking, and acting. That's why it's essential that you practice responding *in the moment* to your anxious or depressed feelings with the workbook skills you've learned. Follow these steps to build and strengthen emotional flexibility in the moment:

1. **Anchor to your breath.** Use your breath to shift out of your head and back into the present moment (chapter 5). Once in the present moment, check your thoughts, your feelings, your actions.

2. **Check your thoughts.** Use the Catch It, Check It, Change It skill (chapter 6). Ask yourself, "What am I thinking? What are the hot automatic thoughts that are intensifying my anxious and depressed feelings? Am I falling into any thinking traps and what are they? Am I jumping to conclusions? Am I catastrophizing? Am I thinking that I won't enjoy an activity before I've even tried it? What flexible thinking strategies could I try now that would help? Are there other ways to interpret events? Are there other ways to think about this that are more reasonable, accurate, or helpful?"

3. **Check your feelings.** Ask yourself, "What am I feeling emotionally and physically? Am I feeling anxious or depressed, or other feelings such as anger, guilt, or shame? Am I hungry, tired, or ill? Are my physical sensations contributing to my anxious or depressed feelings? Am I interpreting my physical situations in a way that intensifies my anxious or depressed feelings? Are these interpretations part of a familiar pattern of inflexible thinking and are they accurate?" Now, FACE your anxious and depressed feelings in the present moment. Observe them as they rise and fall and run their course (chapter 8). Remind yourself that these feelings will pass, as all feelings pass.

4. **Check your actions.** Ask yourself, "Am I feeling the tug to avoid or control my anxious or depressed feelings?" If yes, then resist these emotion-driven avoidance strategies and actions and, when you can, do the opposite. If you're wanting to escape a situation because you feel anxious or down, stay in the situation. If you're checking locks and doors because you're anxious, leave the house and don't look back. If you're saying no to invitations because you predict that you won't enjoy yourself, say yes and set a goal of thirty minutes, or even ten minutes, to see if your prediction is correct.

   Remember, doing the opposite builds your tolerance to anxiety and depression (chapter 8). Also, check whether you're avoiding anxiety or depression in other ways. Ask yourself, "Am I on screens nonstop to distract myself?" If you are, then turn off the device and go for a walk or call a friend, or spend some time with gratitude (chapter 9).

Develop a Practice Plan

A practice plan will help you maintain your recovery over the long term. The plan includes the skills you've learned to enhance the flexibility of your attending, thinking, and acting, and emotion exposure skills to build your emotion tolerance. Since everyone is different, it's likely you've noticed that some skills help you more than other skills. That's okay, but try to practice all the skills from time to time. They're all important, and over time you may discover that those other skills begin to help too.

List the skills you've practiced the most and the skills that have helped the most.

____

____

____

____

____

____

List the skills that you haven't practiced much but would be willing to practice more to see if they help too.

____

____

____

____

____

____

Practice the Plan

The best practice plan in the world won't help if you don't use it. Showing up every day to practice your plan is essential. To that end, make an appointment with yourself to practice, just as if you were making an appointment to meet with a therapist. If you find yourself missing appointments with yourself, you might be slipping into your old avoidance patterns. Heads up!

During each appointment with yourself, review your progress and adjust your practice plan. Remember, the key to managing excessive anxiety and depression over time is to continue to enhance your emotional flexibility. Also note that it's important to practice the workbook skills even when you're not feeling intensely anxious or down—in the same way you take a few practice swings before you actually strike the ball. Practice—any practice—builds and strengthens your emotional flexibility.

Furthermore, if you tend to distract yourself from your emotions or to suppress them, you might actually feel a bit anxious or down without realizing it. Practicing the workbook skills according to a plan rather than just when you feel anxious or down will help you catch your emotional responses before they build to a level where practicing the skills is more difficult—because you're already feeling pretty anxious or down. Use the My Practice Plan to Keep Going Log to track your progress.

My Practice Plan to Keep Going Log

Instructions: Each time you practice one of the workbook skills listed below, check the box. Some skills you'll be able to practice every day, so circle "Today" for those skills. Other skills you'll likely practice several times per week (but not every day), so circle "This Week" for those skills.

Chapter 5: Build Flexible Attention		
Breath as an Anchor	☐☐☐☐☐☐☐☐☐	Today/This Week
Mindfulness of Your Emotions	☐☐☐☐☐☐☐☐☐	Today/This Week
Anchor to Daily Activities	☐☐☐☐☐☐☐☐☐	Today/This Week
Anchor to "And"	☐☐☐☐☐☐☐☐☐	Today/This Week
Anchor to One Thing at a Time	☐☐☐☐☐☐☐☐☐	Today/This Week
Chapter 6: Build Flexible Thinking		
Take the Long Way Around a Thought	☐☐☐☐☐☐☐☐☐	Today/This Week
Catch It, Check It, Change It	☐☐☐☐☐☐☐☐☐	Today/This Week
Test the Accuracy of Your Predictions	☐☐☐☐☐☐☐☐☐	Today/This Week
Calculate Your Validity Quotient	☐☐☐☐☐☐☐☐☐	Today/This Week
View from the Balcony	☐☐☐☐☐☐☐☐☐	Today/This Week
Examine How You Coped in the Past	☐☐☐☐☐☐☐☐☐	Today/This Week
Create a Plan to Jump Back from the Worst	☐☐☐☐☐☐☐☐☐	Today/This Week
Unhook from the Meaning of the Thought	☐☐☐☐☐☐☐☐☐	Today/This Week
Chapter 7: Build Flexible Action		
Understand Emotion Avoidance	☐☐☐☐☐☐☐☐☐	Today/This Week

Practice Alternative Actions	□□□□□□□□□	Today/This Week
Practice Effective Problem Solving	□□□□□□□□□	Today/This Week
Postpone Emotion-Driven Mental Actions	□□□□□□□□□	Today/This Week
Postpone Emotion-Driven Mental Actions in Steps	□□□□□□□□□	Today/This Week
Change Why to How	□□□□□□□□□	Today/This Week
Chapter 8: Build Emotion Tolerance		
Practice Physical Sensation Exposure	□□□□□□□□□	Today/This Week
Practice External Situation Emotion Exposure	□□□□□□□□□	Today/This Week
Practice Internal Situation Emotion Exposure	□□□□□□□□□	Today/This Week
Chapter 9: Build Gratitude and Self-Compassion		
Keep a Gratitude Journal	□□□□□□□□□	Today/This Week
Write Thank-You Notes	□□□□□□□□□	Today/This Week
Meditate on Gratitude	□□□□□□□□□	Today/This Week
Write a Compassionate Letter to Yourself	□□□□□□□□□	Today/This Week
Hand on Heart	□□□□□□□□□	Today/This Week
Meditate on Loving-Kindness	□□□□□□□□□	Today/This Week
Keep a Self-Compassion Journal	□□□□□□□□□	Today/This Week
Take a Self-Compassion Break	□□□□□□□□□	Today/This Week

Remember to Step Toward Discomfort

Perhaps there's no more important part of your practice plan than looking for opportunities to step toward discomfort. These are the emotion exposures you've practiced. Increasing your emotion tolerance through approaching rather than retreating from your anxious and depressed feelings (as well as other feelings, such as guilt or shame) is essential to maintaining your recovery. Look at the Emotion Exposure Planning Worksheets you developed in chapter 8. Include in your practice plan the top third of each of your emotion exposure ladders, and practice at least two or three of these every day.

You might wonder why repeating what you've already mastered would keep your recovery going. Well, you'll likely notice that even the steps in the ladders that you've mastered and which no longer make you uncomfortable will feel a little harder when you're feeling more stressed or upset by some life event. That's because day-to-day stress can make everything a little harder, including stepping toward your anxious and depressed feelings. Remember, although you'll get the most out of practices when you're feeling a bit more anxious or down, even when you're not, you're still building a habit—the habit of approaching rather than retreating from your emotions.

Prepare for New Symptoms

Regardless of the progress you've made, life has a way of presenting challenges that will bump up your anxiety or push down your mood. Moving to a new city, taking a new job, and the loss of a friend or loved one are examples of the challenges of life. At these times, you might observe a new symptom—a new image, a new thought, perhaps a new emotion-driven action.

Don't be alarmed by new symptoms. A new symptom doesn't mean that you've fallen back into the emotional inflexibility that you've worked so hard to escape. At the same time, you don't want to ignore new symptoms. Instead, practice the skills you've learned with these new symptoms. Even though they might look and feel different, they're a piece of the same old pattern of inflexible attending, thinking, and acting. The skills you've learned will help with these symptoms too.

Chart Your Path to a Fuller Life

Excessive anxious and depressed feelings have a way of taking people's lives off course. Now that you've completed this workbook and you're feeling less anxious and depressed, it's time to reflect on unfulfilled dreams and desires, and chart your path to a fuller life. Perhaps, as you've practiced the skills you've learned, you're closer now than you were before to accomplishing what you set out to do. Recovery is a marathon, not a sprint, and it's time for you to review what you've accomplished and develop a new plan to take you the rest of the way.

Take a moment to review the values (chapter 4) that started you along the path to a fuller life. Are you closer now to meeting the long-term goals that are consistent with your personal values? Have you started dating? Have you flown to Greece on that trip that you've been talking about for years? Have you left that dead-end job and found a new one?

Look at Nia's Chart My Path to a Fuller Life Worksheet. She decided to focus on her core value—work and career—because so much of her anxiety centered on feeling stuck in a dead-end job. In order to honor her core value, she decided to work toward finding a job teaching children math and science, subjects she has always loved. She then plotted out the steps to achieve this goal. Interestingly, Nia felt less overwhelmed by the task of finding a teaching job when she plotted it out step by step. That's often the case. Charting the path to a fuller life makes what seems overwhelming and undoable into something that you can accomplish with effort and work.

Nia's Chart My Path to a Fuller Life Worksheet

Value	Work and career: I want to have a job that helps children.
Long-Term Goal	Get a job teaching children math and science.
Steps to Achieve My Long-Term Goal	
Complete teacher certification in math and science.	Step 1
Call the school district and apply for teaching internship.	Step 2
Complete résumé and get letters of reference.	Step 3
Submit application for teaching internship.	Step 4
Complete teaching internship.	Step 5
File papers for teaching certificate.	Step 6
Redo résumé and apply for teaching jobs in local schools.	Step 7
Work as a substitute teacher until I find a permanent teaching job.	Step 8
Long-Term Goal	Get a job teaching children math and science.

Now, chart your own path to a fuller life. Begin with a core value and let your values lead the way toward achieving a long-term goal. You might discover that your path includes more than the eight steps on the worksheet. Break down the steps to achieve the long-term goal into as many steps as you like.

In fact, the more steps you build into your plan, the smaller each step becomes, which can decrease feelings of overwhelm or discouragement. Furthermore, each step, no matter how small, is an opportunity to practice what you've learned in this workbook. Knowing your value-driven path, as well as what to do to help you along the way, is the best way to achieve long-term goals.

Chart My Path to a Fuller Life Worksheet

Value	
Long-Term Goal	

Steps to Achieve My Long-Term Goal	
	Step 1
	Step 2
	Step 3
	Step 4
	Step 5
	Step 6
	Step 7
	Step 8

Long-Term Goal	

Long Story Short

Building and maintaining emotional flexibility is central to emotional well-being and to emotional responses that enable you to move through life's day-to-day challenges. Although your emotional system is more flexible now, it's essential that you remain vigilant for signs that you're slowly slipping back into the old inflexible and automatic patterns that you've worked so hard to escape, so remember:

- Remain vigilant for signs that you're slipping into old patterns of attending, thinking, and acting. The sooner you can apply the skills you've learned, the sooner you'll recover.
- Review your Practice Plan to Keep Going Log frequently and practice the skills in the plan regularly. In particular, practice stepping toward discomfort because discomfort is an inescapable part of a life well lived.
- Reconnect with the core values that helped you recover from your excessive anxiety or depression. Follow those values to pursue the long-term life goals that you set aside because you thought you were too anxious or depressed to accomplish them.

Acknowledgments

I thank my wife, Luann DeVoss, and our daughters, Madeleine and Olivia, for their unwavering support of another book project.

I thank my colleagues at the San Francisco Bay Area Center for Cognitive Therapy (Jonathan Barkin, Emily Berner, Joan Davidson, Daniela Owen, and Monique Thompson) for their continued support of my professional development. I also thank Judy Beck and Jackie Persons. I am fortunate to call these rock stars of cognitive behavioral therapy my colleagues and friends.

I thank Tesilya Hanauer, my editor at New Harbinger Publications. We have worked together on several book projects over the years, and Tesilya is always thoughtful, patient, and generous in her support and guidance. I also thank Vicraj Gill for her thoughtful suggestions that greatly improved the manuscript.

References

Allen, L. B., R. K. McHugh, and D. H. Barlow. 2008. "Emotional Disorders: A Unified Protocol." In *Clinical Handbook of Psychological Disorders: A Step-by-Step Treatment Manual*. 4th ed. Edited by D. H. Barlow. New York: Guilford Press.

American Psychiatric Association. 2013. *Diagnostic and Statistical Manual of Mental Disorders*. 5th ed. Arlington, VA: American Psychiatric Publishing.

Brown, T. A., and D. H. Barlow. 2009. "A Proposal for a Dimensional Classification System Based on the Shared Features of the DSM-IV Anxiety and Mood Disorders: Implications for Assessment and Treatment." *Psychological Assessment* 21: 256–271.

Burns, D. D. 1980. *Feeling Good: The New Mood Therapy*. New York: Signet.

Ellard, K. K., C. P. Fairholme, C. L. Boisseau, T. J. Farchione, and D. H. Barlow. 2010. "Unified Protocol for the Transdiagnostic Treatment of Emotional Disorders: Protocol Development and Initial Outcome Data." *Cognitive and Behavioral Practice* 17 (1): 88–101.

Farchione, T. J., C. P. Fairholme, K. K. Ellard, C. L. Boisseau, J. Thompson-Hollands, J. R. Carl, M. W. Gallagher, and D. H. Barlow. 2012. "The Unified Protocol for the Transdiagnostic Treatment of Emotional Disorders: A Randomized Controlled Trial." *Behavior Therapy* 3: 666–678.

Hasin, D., A. L. Sarvet, J. L. Meyers, T. D. Saha, W. J. Ruan, M. Stohl, and B. F. Grant. 2017. "Epidemiology of Adult DSM-5 Major Depressive Disorder and Its Specifiers in the United States." *Journal of the American Medical Association* 75 (4): 336–346.

Kaufman, J., and D. Charney. 2000. "Comorbidity of Mood and Anxiety Disorders." *Depression and Anxiety* 12 (Supplement 1): 69–76.

Moses, E. B., and D. H. Barlow. 2006. "A New Unified Treatment Approach for Emotional Disorders Based on Emotion Science." *Current Directions in Psychological Science* 15 (3): 146–150.

Norton, P. J., and D. J. Paulus. 2016. "Toward a Unified Treatment for Emotional Disorders: Update on the Science and Practice." *Behavior Therapy* 47 (6): 854–868.

Regier, D. A., D. S. Rae, W. E. Narrow, C. T. Kaelber, and A. F. Schatzberg. 1998. "Prevalence of Anxiety Disorders and Their Comorbidity with Mood and Addictive Disorders." *British Journal of Psychiatry* 173 (Supplement 34): 24–28.

Taylor, S., and D. A. Clark. 2009. "Transdiagnostic Cognitive-Behavioral Treatments for Mood and Anxiety Disorders: Introduction to the Special Issue." *Journal of Cognitive Psychotherapy: An International Quarterly* 23: 3–5.

Michael A. Tompkins, PhD, ABPP, is a board-certified psychologist in behavioral and cognitive psychology. He is codirector of the San Francisco Bay Area Center for Cognitive Therapy; and assistant clinical professor of psychology at the University of California, Berkeley. Tompkins is author or coauthor of twelve books, including five books published by New Harbinger. Tompkins has presented over 600 workshops, lectures, and keynote addresses on cognitive behavioral therapy (CBT) and related topics nationally and internationally. He is an adjunct faculty member of the Beck Institute for Cognitive Behavior Therapy.

Foreword writer **Judith S. Beck, PhD**, is director of the Beck Institute for Cognitive Behavior Therapy, and past president of the Academy of Cognitive Therapy. Daughter of influential founder of cognitive therapy, Aaron T. Beck, Beck is author of *The Beck Diet Solution*.

FROM OUR PUBLISHER—

As the publisher at New Harbinger and a clinical psychologist since 1978, I know that emotional problems are best helped with evidence-based therapies. These are the treatments derived from scientific research (randomized controlled trials) that show what works. Whether these treatments are delivered by trained clinicians or found in a self-help book, they are designed to provide you with proven strategies to overcome your problem.

Therapies that aren't evidence-based—whether offered by clinicians or in books—are much less likely to help. In fact, therapies that aren't guided by science may not help you at all. That's why this New Harbinger book is based on scientific evidence that the treatment can relieve emotional pain.

This is important: if this book isn't enough, and you need the help of a skilled therapist, use the following resources to find a clinician trained in the evidence-based protocols appropriate for your problem. And if you need more support—a community that understands what you're going through and can show you ways to cope—resources for that are provided below, as well.

Real help is available for the problems you have been struggling with. The skills you can learn from evidence-based therapies will change your life.

Matthew McKay, PhD
Publisher, New Harbinger Publications

If you need a therapist, the following organization can help you find a therapist trained in cognitive behavioral therapy (CBT).

The Association for Behavioral & Cognitive Therapies (ABCT) Find-a-Therapist service offers a list of therapists schooled in CBT techniques. Therapists listed are licensed professionals who have met the membership requirements of ABCT and who have chosen to appear in the directory.

Please visit www.abct.org and click on *Find a Therapist*.

For additional support for patients, family, and friends, contact the following:

Anxiety and Depression Association of American (ADAA)
visit www.adaa.org

National Alliance on Mental Illness (NAMI)
please visit www.nami.org

National Suicide Prevention Lifeline
Call 24 hours a day 1-800-273-TALK (8255) or visit www.suicidepreventionlifeline.org

new harbinger
CELEBRATING
40 YEARS